Remembering a
Forgotten Grace

Dedicated to:
Craig and Diane Tucker
Dr. Rick McPeak and Team Nanning

Remembering a Forgotten Grace

Thoughts on Shame, Beauty, Romance and Radiance

by

Roderick M. Tucker

Hope Publishing House
Pasadena, California

For information address:

Hope Publishing House
P.O. Box 60008
Pasadena, CA 91116 - U.S.A.
Tel: (626) 792-6123 / Fax: (626) 792-2121
E-mail: hopepub@sbcglobal.net
Web site: http://www.hope-pub.com

Printed on acid-free paper
Cover design — Michael McClary/The Workshop

Library of Congress Cataloging-in-Publication Data

Tucker, Roderick M., 1982–
    Remembering a forgotten grace : thoughts on shame, beauty, romance, and radiance / by Roderick M. Tucker.-- 1st. ed.
        p. cm.
    Part One: The art of disgrace -- Names -- Coverings -- Fame -- Naked -- Choices -- Glory -- Illumination -- Hungry -- Part Two: The forgotten grace -- Body -- Striving -- Church -- Excellence -- Bob -- Unity -- Titles -- Perfection -- Grace -- Part Three: The Bride of Christ -- Newness -- Feet -- Constant -- Heart -- Dreams -- Part Four: Joy in mourning -- Jesus -- Sex -- Trust -- Joy.
    Includes bibliographical references.
    ISBN-13: 978-1-932717-14-3 (trade pbk. : alk. paper)
    ISBN-10: 1-932717-14-5 (alk. paper)
    1. Teenagers- -Religious life. 2. Tucker, Roderick, 1982- I. Title.
    BV4531.3.T83 2008
    248.8'3--dc22
                                                            2007044107

Contents

Acknowledgments vi

Author's Note vii

Introduction viii

Part One: The Art of Disgrace

   1 – Names 2

   2 – Coverings 5

   3 – Fame 10

   4 – Naked 12

   5 – Choices 17

   6 – Glory 21

   7 – Illumination 26

   8 – Hungry 30

Part Two: The Forgotten Grace

   9 – Body 40

  10 – Striving 46

  11 – Church 52

  12 – Excellence 58

  13 – Bob 64

  14 – Unity 66

  15 – Titles 68

  16 – Perfection 70

  17 – Grace 72

Part Three: The Bride of Christ

  18 – Newness 76

  19 – Feet 85

  20 – Constant 93

  21 – Heart 99

  22 – Dreams 106

Part Four: Joy in Mourning

  23 – Jesus 114

  24 – Sex 122

  25 – Trust 128

  26 – Joy 132

Epilogue 141

Bibliography 143

Acknowledgments

I would like to thank the many people who have read this book and told me what they thought. First I would like to thank Hope Publishing House for providing me a venue to share my reflections. My family has been a huge support and I am grateful for our lives together. Jason Haak, thanks for being the smartest person I know; Jeremy Deimund, my best friend. Chris Scott, you are my shout-out guy. Here is your shout-out. Amanda Reese, thanks for all your hard work. Janice Adamek, I could not have gotten this book published without your help. My sisters, Lisa, Christie and Kelly, I love you all. Dad and Mom, you guys wrote this book just as much as I did. I love you. Randy Thomspon, may we learn to be good writers. Chris Hohm and Emily Bishop, thanks for helping with the artwork. Dr. Rick McPeak, thanks for teaching me about community. Team Nanning, thanks for showing me how true community manifests itself in this world. To all those whom I have met along this journey we call life, thanks for inspiring me to be me and loving me as I learned to be myself. I love you all and wait in eager expectation for eternity, which will be spent together.

—Rod *(roderickmtucker@yahoo.com)*

Author's Note

Sometimes in our lives, what seems to be the most controversial ideas are those ideas which not only challenge us the most, but also have potential to change us for the most good if we allow ourselves to stop arguing with all that we disagree and listen to what these ideas have to say. May the Lord help us as we move from a modern deliberation to a new land where stories reign free and truth is no longer hidden behind the agenda of superfluous religious conviction.

My purpose in writing this book was to tell a story that might possibly challenge those whose eyes scan the words on its pages. I did not write an argument. I wrote a story. My intention was not to convince others of anything so that they might consent to my way of thinking, or rally around my book. I wrote this book to connect in a simple way your story, my story and the story of all humanity (past and present), as we discover and hope for what life is like on the other side of shame.

Introduction

My last year of college I had to turn in a statement of faith for my senior capstone class and final exam. Scared of what grade I might receive I turned in a painting. It was orange, black, red, and yellow splattered across a frame and a backing which I had found near a dumpster a couple days before. I wrote my name in white on the black backing of the painting and turned it in, leaning my work against my teacher's door. A week later I received an A. This was one of the most powerful moments in my life. Consequently, this book is partially dedicated to the man who helped teach me to think in languages other than mine own.

What surprised me most about my piece was really nothing that I had done. A year later as I was sitting in this man's office discussing the work with him I mentioned why I had written my name in white on the back. He smiled and told me that was how he had actually been hanging my painting, backwards. In that moment I felt understood. I felt loved. I felt grace.

I live my life in awe of people, like my professor, who never see others at face value. He has understanding of grace that I believe you only learn to attain as you learn to love people like myself.

I hope that you enjoy this book. The words are yours as much as they are mine. Thanks for sharing in this story.

Remembering a Forgotten Grace

Part One

The Art of Disgrace

1

Names

There comes a time in all of our lives when we must tell God that He is worth more to us than our own notions of love.

"Hello, my name is Rod and I'm a child of an alcoholic." The words echo in my mind as I hear each person in the gathering unravel a reality explaining why they have come seeking restoration from an Alcoholics Anonymous meeting. It is my parents' turn, and then mine, "Hello, my name is Rod and I'm a child of an alcoholic."

"Hi Rod."

Hearing those words, "Hi Rod," bring back memories that cause me to question why the world today does not refer to us by our names. Whether it is Alcoholic or a multitude of other names that do not define who we really are, we are called these names and it hurts. At this moment, the world is standing in a doorway between what is real and what is being experienced. A hope for freedom lies in the desire to hear the voice of someone who is daring enough to call us by our true names.

Do you know what your name is?

We all have pain in our lives. Many experiences have driven our emotions, wills, minds and spirits into places that deep down, in our inmost beings, we wish we had never known. The problem that arises from these circumstances is no one wants to admit their pain has determined who they believe they are.

A story is told in Alcoholics Anonymous of a young man attending a meeting who would not admit having a problem with alcohol. His problem may have originated in a variety of ways. Maybe his father was an alcoholic or maybe he began drinking socially and slowly fell into alcohol's cunning grip. In any case, this young man was not budging. As everyone in the meeting addressed the problem of addiction (which obviously possessed this young man) he became more defensive, convinced that given any situation, when asked to stop drinking he could put the bottle down and never again take another drink.

Realizing this debate was going nowhere, an elderly man stood up, pointed his finger directly at the young man and said, "Son, what you need to do is to get up, leave this meeting, go to the next bar you come across and buy yourself a drink. After you are finished with that drink buy yourself another, and another, and another. Stay at that bar until you realize the truth. When you come to agree with the rest of us that there is a problem, come back. Then, and only then, will you begin to work through your issues, together with us, as a group."

Just like this young man, we all have pain in our lives which can lead us to negative coping, such as drinking and drugs. Usually this pain drives us into corners of our very own beings that we did not know even existed. Often we feel as though we would have been better off had we never known there even was a problem. Nevertheless, we run to a buffet of psychiatrists and counselors in order to learn how to "just let it go." The problem is that, in all honesty, we do not even know what we are holding onto and "letting it go" is what we have been doing our entire lives. I am not talking about alcoholism when I say that one has a problem. In fact, I am not even talking about low self-esteem. What I am talking about is shame, an identity crisis.

Unlike the feeling of conviction or guilt, shame is the belief that we are the problem – not the belief that we have caused a problem but that we are the problem and need to be fixed. Neil T. Anderson writes in his book, *Breaking the Bondage of Legalism* that "Guilt is the sense that you have done something wrong. Shame is the sense that you are the something that is wrong" (2003:15). Shame has been a driving force in humanity since Adam and Eve first violated God's rules in the Garden of Eden and people everywhere need to grasp this because "letting it go" is causing more problems than most of us even know!

Freedom from shame lies in the truth that all knowledge of ourselves and ideas of who we are, is to be made captive to the Creator of the universe. The Bible commands us to, "Take every thought captive to make it obedient to Christ" (2 Co 10:5b), not "let it go," not forget about it, but take it captive and make it compliant to all that God says we are because of His Son. In order to do this we must first discover where shame began, since our story is no different from all people's, and from there we must send our knowledge to Jesus. Gripping the reality of shame rather than experiencing shame's effects brings the freedom to be okay, and this all begins with acknowledging where the problem began: Genesis chapter three.

2

Coverings

I remember playing basketball with my friends when I was in the third grade. I had never played it before but as I wandered around the court, my friends told each other who they were going to play as, and I knew how critical it was for me to pick a good player. "I'm Michael Jordan!" I shouted, but it was too late, he was one of the first ones to be picked. "Well how about Scottie Pippin?" I asked. Nope, he was taken too. I was lost. Those were the only two players in the NBA that I had ever heard of before. "Man," I thought, "if I'm not anybody...what will I do?" At that moment the feeling of being unaccepted might have been one of the worst feelings I'd ever experienced. However, one of my friends came to my rescue. "You can be Jon Paxon; he's good." "Whew, I get to be somebody good," I thought. All of a sudden there was no more shame. A good friend had taken the extra time needed to make sure I was acceptable.

"Then the eyes of both of them were opened, and they realized they were naked" (Gen 3:7a).

From the beginning, the focus of human life has been on shame. Adam and Eve sinned and at the moment when they realized that nothing done out of human ability could make them better than who God had uniquely designed them to be, they realized that they were naked. Adam and Eve no longer allowed God to tell them who they were. Instead, they tried to become gods themselves. To be created in the image of God and then be deceived into believing that they were defective is where shame began for Adam and Eve; this is the same place where shame begins in people's lives everywhere.

The problem with the lie of shame is that it does not just start with the feeling of being insignificant. Shame says, "You are the reason that you're insignificant. Fix yourself." Shame does not only confuse our emotions, it tells us that if we don't fix everything (including our own feelings) we will never be acceptable. Like Adam and Eve, we attempt to make ourselves better and thus we relinquish to shame an increasing influence over our lives. All the while God has given us a Friend who has made us acceptable. We need to quit trying to rid ourselves of this shame and discover what it really means to be clothed in Christ.

"So they sewed fig leaves together and made coverings for themselves" (Gen. 3:7b).

I can remember one of the first times that I found myself in trouble with my parents. I had done something that I knew I should not have done, like coloring with crayons on the floor, but it was too late. I quickly attempted to find a way to make everything just as it was before I had screwed it all up. Usually covering the shame that I felt involved some sort of pretending. When my parents would come home and ask me how I was, I would respond by saying something like, "I'm fine and I didn't do anything." Well, those fig leaves did not hold up very long against the radar of my seemingly omniscient parents. They would respond by saying, "Rod, what did you do?" At that very second (and it happened this way every single time) I would be faced with what I like to call a moment of truth. Little did I know that if I confessed and told the truth, I would be forgiven and set free of the shame I was experiencing. Instead, I tried once again to cover my shame

Remembering a Forgotten Grace

and make myself better by pointing the finger at someone else. That someone else just happened to be my sister who was usually more than ready to tell my parents what had really happened. In an attempt to cover my shame I had now created an even larger problem for myself. I had lied. Being real before my parents was the last thing that I wanted to do and, because I could not be real, my shame only worsened, just like with Adam and Eve. So where did we learn to cover our shame instead of being real with God? That's right, Adam and Eve, the people with whom this horrible cycle began.

The story of Adam and Eve told in Genesis goes like this: Adam and Eve were hanging out in the Garden of Eden naked and unashamed before God. Why were they naked and unashamed? First of all, they had not yet sinned. Second, neither one of their focuses was on themselves; their eyes were fixed on their Creator and God's wonderful creation. Then, just like the story says, they both (not just Eve) wandered over by the Tree of Knowledge of Good and Evil, the very tree from which God told them not to eat. Well, the whole wandering thing would not have been such a big deal if it hadn't been for the third party who just happened also to be enjoying the view from under that particular tree. The serpent knew that if he could convince these two to eat from the only tree forbidden by God, then the just God that he knew would be required to punish them for their sin, or else God would not be a God of justice. The serpent also knew firsthand what happens to individuals who go against Almighty God: they are cast from God's presence.

So what did this crafty serpent do? First of all, he skipped over any small talk that had even the possibility of bringing God praise and said to Eve, "Did God really say, 'You must not eat from any tree in the garden'?" Eve told the serpent, "We may eat fruit from the trees in the garden, but God did say, 'You must not eat fruit from the tree that is in the middle of the garden and you must not touch it, or you will die.'"

For the first time and definitely not the last, conversation began between those created in the image of God and a serpent. Even after the conversation started, Eve's mistake was not her first answer to the serpent – which was the same kind of answer we need to learn to give for Eve answered with the words of God. But ultimately Eve did not resist and Adam said nothing. They, like we, sinned.

I have heard many preachers explain that the problem was Adam and Eve's inability to resist temptation. It almost seems the gospel for these teachers is more a prescription for avoiding sin than an opportunity to receive grace and begin transcending oneself. This can create a dangerous situation for both the teachers of this doctrine and the hearers. The serpent was probably the first teacher to use such deceptive principles. The dogma began with telling Adam and Eve they needed this prescription if they were to be like God and know in the same way God knows.

The marketing of this illusory teaching was simple and it ended in shame. "For God knows that when you eat of it your eyes will be opened and you will be like God, knowing good and evil" (Gen. 3:5).

Shame usually begins with pride. The serpent basically told Adam and Eve they could improve their status by telling them, "You're not good enough, but you can fix yourself. Eat this fruit and you will be like God." This lie never stops with just telling us that we are not good enough; the goal is to give us more than just low self-esteem. This lie wants to destroy our very selves in whom Christ has hidden His very own glory. It doesn't stop with us feeling bad. It tells us we can fix ourselves and each time we try, the influence of shame grows more and more, convincing us that we are the problem.

Adam and Eve ate the fruit and then they noticed that they

were naked. Here is where a definite problem lies. They always had been naked! Genesis tells us., "The man and his wife were both naked and they felt no shame" (2:25). So what is the big deal with realizing that they were naked? The difference is shame. After Adam and Eve had eaten the fruit, "Then the eyes of both of them were opened and they realized they were naked; so they sewed fig leaves together and made coverings for themselves" (Gen 3:7).

Before sin entered the world Adam and Eve were both naked without shame. After it had manifested itself in their lives, Adam and Eve realized they were naked and then they were ashamed. So because Adam and Ever were deceived into believing they were not good enough, they took the bait and tried to improve their lot in life and subsequently fell into a cycle of shame. The next round, however, Adam and Eve found themselves not trying to make themselves better than how God had created them, for they knew that was impossible. They tried to un-realize their newly discovered nakedness and in so doing, Adam and Eve's attempt to fix themselves and disconnect their own shame made itself apparent in nothing more than a cluster of fig leaves that could not cover what they knew to be true about their bodies.

Adam and Eve were covered in shame. Once they sinned, they began looking only at themselves and each other. Their eyes were no longer fixed on God.

3

Fame

The serpent initially twisted Adam and Eve's concept of God's glory by telling them that glory was fame and that they could become people greater than how God had created them. The truth is, glory is not about us having to correct our current state of being. Luminosity, glory defined, is about nothing more than being noticed by God.

C.S. Lewis writes in *The Weight of Glory* "Either Glory means to me fame, or it means luminosity. As for the first, since to be famous means to be better known than other people [or God Himself], the desire for fame appears to me as a competitive passion and therefore of hell rather than heaven." Then he explains: "As for the second, who wishes to become a kind of living electric light bulb?" (2001:36).

Few people, it would appear, have ever thought to describe the Glory of God using words like radiant, luminous, illuminating or even bright. It would seem we have all been deceived into believing God's glory is about being famous and not about being blinded. One can see this when we read about a mother's request for her two sons:

Then the mother of Zebedee's sons came to Jesus with her sons and, kneeling down, asked a favor of him. "What is it you want?" he asked. She said, "Grant that one of these two sons of mine may sit at your right and the other at your left in your kingdom." "You don't know what you are asking," Jesus said to them. "Can you drink the cup I am going to drink?" (Mt 20:20-22).

Obviously, God is the only "Famous One" as the song says, because to be "The Famous One" God must be seen as greater than all. Any other definition or form of this word is a far cry from how God intended it. King David said in 1 Chronicles 22:5 that a house built for the Lord should be great in magnificence, fame and glory. But true fame and true glory need to be defined in two different ways. One, God is famous. He is above all things. Two, God is glorious. He is the creator and giver of an illuminating light in which there can be no shame. God is and has always been luminous, but for some reason we all want to be something greater than we are in the hopes that we will somehow attain a "god-like" persona, or – if we are not that far off of our rockers – at least some form of glory. We do this in order to cover our shame. This is an extremely monotonous way of sewing fig leaves that can be traced all the way back to pharaohs, emperors and individuals such as Napoleon.

Ultimately I feel that fame is a lie. In our culture this is especially difficult because it seems the most popular way of covering shame is by becoming the most popular. Perhaps believing we are the problem, we then believe we can mask who we believe ourselves to be by becoming famous, something we are most definitely not. If fame is truly a lie, than perhaps all being famous does is cause more eyes to focus on us for what we are not. So if we are famous in the eyes of our culture, maybe we have done something to make ourselves look or be perceived as something other than what we believe ourselves to be and we have done whatever is necessary to accomplish this task better than everyone else around us. Thus fame makes us incapable of being honest with ourselves, others and God. This is a choice that we have made.

4

Naked

Sometimes I wonder if through understanding ourselves, we, like Adam and Eve, strive to figure out ways to replace the cloud of shame on our faces with the illumination that comes from the Glory of God. Intuitively we know that radiance is being offered to us and that if we can only obtain this illumination, our lives might be changed forever. We know who holds our joy but we act as if we have been to Him before, but returned wanting every single time. Somehow we convince ourselves that the shame we experience daily is some kind of "thorn in the flesh" which will never go away. Perhaps carrying our cross in this life means learning to live with the belief we are illegitimate children of God. We might never admit to this notion, but ultimately we hold that even though Christ died for our sins and covered us with His blood, we are still the problem with this world.

Our past is covered with clouds of memories from which we have tried desperately to hide. We have convinced ourselves that if we only try hard enough, we will eventually change and our past will be forgotten. However, we find that trying to forget our past is like trying to swim our way out of the middle of the ocean. The more we try to leave our past the more of it we find haunting us. Every day that has turned into yesterday has caused more

Remembering a Forgotten Grace

shame to pile onto the very lives we are trying to change. We find ourselves asking God, "Why did you make me like this?"

We hear sermon after sermon about how God says we are beautiful. This doesn't help our situation because we have already reached the conclusion that even though the Bible says beauty is on the inside, we desire with almost everything that is in us to be attractive—so that someone will notice us—even if it is only one person. We have fallen for the temptation to be sexy. Even though we know this is wrong, we have convinced ourselves it is better to be inappropriate and sexy than to be of good character and ugly. Makeup has failed to cover the cloud of shame we know is over our faces and, the more we put on in attempts to become lovely, the more we feel as though we are fake.

For many of us food has become our conquering enemy, no matter how much we have purged ourselves of its evil. We desire deep down to be filled with something that can make us beautiful. In our hearts we know that true radiance comes from having a real relationship with the very being from whom we are hiding. We dream of running to Him, falling into His arms and letting Him tell us who we are; all the while we are in His presence. We long to hear the words that will tell us of how dauntlessly we have been pursued and how we are being swept off of our feet. But we do not go to Him. In fact, we dare not go. We believe we are not real, but that we are fake. We know that if we go before our Creator covered in the shame that we have brought upon ourselves we will be laid bare, open with no covering and clouded with no radiance. From childhood on, we hide in fear of what we might have become. All of this time we have not known what our Father thinks of us and we have not recognized that He has never stopped calling our name wanting to get our attention.

Many of us do not know what it means to "be real." We believe that if we work hard enough or exercise enough we will find the secret to success, which we believe is found in one's ability to achieve. We are told from day one that a real individual does not cry and that feelings are something with which only the weak struggle. We do not believe that meekness is where true power and authority are defined. We are afraid of being rejects, the ones turned away because we are of inferior quality. Because of this fear, many of us live our lives in shame and we are unable to lay bare before the Lord, remembering times that we over-exerted our power. During those remembered times we were convinced that force was the only way to prove that we had a voice. Deep down this is what we truly believe. Constant apologies to our peers do nothing to remove the cloud of shame that is covering our faces. We fear that, because we are the problem, the next time trouble comes we will once again become angry and hurt the ones who are most precious to us. We have fought for acceptance and have failed to all those against whom we have fought.

We do not know how to be humble, because glory and radiance to us is fame. Fame causes the most shame-filled competition among people. In reality, our struggle has never been against each other, but is against the one who wants nothing more than to tell us the only way in which we will ever be desired is if we achieve for ourselves the world's definition of acceptance, which is many times nothing more than control over everyone and everything around us. We do not want to go before a Holy God, because we know that is when everything is laid bare and all of our failures are shown. Our feeble attempts to become all of what God has designed us to be have failed miserably. Shame that comes from sexual immorality, idolatry, greed, jealousy and every form of sin that we have found ourselves unable to resist because of our failures, causes us to believe we are once again the problems.

The problem with shame is that we have not been real with God in the first place. We have been given chance after chance to stand before God as all that we are and have become, turning our eyes to Him, but because we know no other ways to get the focus off ourselves we blame. Our fig leaves have proven to be less than adequate in covering our bare nakedness and we have been found hiding. God is asking us, "What has happened?" and instead of being real, we point the finger, pushing shame onto others and receiving it from them in return.

Shame has obviously embedded itself into our lives and thoughts so much, we have failed even to recognize its existence. We go about our lives assuming we are some kind of complex problem that may never be solved. Sure, we may have placed our faith in Christ but as Christians we wonder why we must battle these feelings of inadequacy each and every day. We tell ourselves that these feelings should have disappeared when we "gave it all to Jesus," but since they have not, we accept the lie that we are just not as "mature in Christ" as other believers around us. We find ourselves fighting the most difficult battle of our lives. We have been fighting in order to prove ourselves worthy to others and to God. We have done this in hope that we will be accepted and loved as something more than what we have come to believe we are in a world that is doing the exact same thing as us, searching for glory and, all the while, covering itself in shame.

The time to be real with God is now and the time of seeing the wall of shame crumble in our own lives will come when we are real with God. "Come to me, all you who are weary and burdened and I will give you rest" (Mt 11:28). We do not have to fight anymore. The Bible tells us Adam and Eve became ashamed when their eyes were opened and they realized they were naked. There are two different words used for the English word "naked" in Genesis 2:25: "The man and his wife were both naked and they felt no shame," and Genesis 3:7a: "Then the eyes of both of them were opened and they realized they were naked." The word translated from Genesis 2:25 is originally from the Hebrew word "aw rome" which means nothing more than partially or totally nude. In Adam and Eve's case it is assumed the two were totally nude and unashamed. But in Genesis 3:7 the word used is "ay-rome" which means much more than just being in the nude, for it means to be naked and laid bare. In other words, Adam and Eve were not only revealed as naked but as lacking the appropriate covering. To be undisguised before God after having just committed their first sin left the two swimming in more shame than they could have ever imagined.

In a matter of moments Adam and Eve went from being so right before God to being the problem. They believed there was no way in which they would ever be able to approach their Father without some sort of covering; so they started sewing. When the fig leaves didn't hold up, Adam and Eve decided it would be a good idea to hide and that is exactly what they did.

They were faced with their first opportunities to be real, or open and honest, with God, but instead of coming out and telling God they had sinned, they tried to deceive God with fig leaves which only brought more shame upon themselves. When that did not work, Adam and Eve hid from God in fear of their own nakedness, which was now being laid bare. So with the first two opportunities having been soundly rejected by God's first two humans, what did God do? One might imagine that in His own righteousness, justice, anger and wrath, God kicked Adam and Eve out of the Garden of Eden without a second thought. However, that is not what He did. Believe it or not, God actually gave Adam and Eve one last opportunity to be real with Him. All that they would have had to do was confess. Remember 1 John 1:9? "If we confess our sins He is faithful and just to forgive us our sins and purify us from all unrighteousness." Adam and Eve didn't want to be real with God. They had allowed shame to control them so much that the only way in which they knew to remove the focus from themselves was to point the finger at each other. Instead of confessing, Adam and Eve started blaming and that is when judgment came.

5

Choices

"The more they increased, the more they sinned against me; I will change their glory into shame" (Hos 4:7).

Sinning against God brings shame because it causes us to become something other than what God has initially designed us to become. You and I were created to represent the Glory of God in one of its purest forms and we sinned. Not only did this cause us to become un-glorifiable, it also shamed us so we were disgraced before our Creator. We were never the problem, sin was, but we were filled with the problem when we became sinful people. Sin entered our bodies corrupting our ability to choose God, but, know this, we are not our choices. There is a difference between being sinful and shameful.

Although designed to distract people from true glory, shame has been used by God since the fall of man to show sinful humans they are unworthy or disgraced before Him and His glory. It is safe to claim everybody is either currently living or has lived under the rule of shame. Romans 3:23 says, "All have sinned and fall short of the glory of God." So if sin has caused us to fall short of living under and experiencing God's glory, what are we living beneath now? Exactly. When not clothed in the glory of God we appear disgraced and that is what shame is all about.

God warns Ezekiel the people of Israel's faces will be covered with shame and that "They will throw their silver into the streets and their gold will be an unclean thing. Their silver and gold will not be able to save them in the day of the Lord's wrath....They were proud of their beautiful jewelry and used it to make their detestable idols and vile images" (7:19a, 20a). Wow! Proud of their jewelry, detestable idols, vile images! Sounds pretty scary. You probably agree and say, "If I were the Lord, I would unleash my wrath upon Israel too!" Before you do that, answer me one question: What makes a woman beautiful? Take your time to think up your answer, but while you are thinking about this, ask yourself: Am I proud of what the world is calling beautiful? Have I set things up as idols making them a higher priority than God? How much makeup is enough? Am I viewing vile images and allowing them to control my life?

The problem comes from not understanding that the actions which we take to overcome or cover up our disgracefulness are the very actions that caused us to be covered in shame. The process explained in this Ezekiel passage is simple. Israel sinned – setting up idols above God – and shame was the result. This is a vicious and venomous cycle. We need to ask ourselves, "If I am experiencing shame in my life, do I need to deal with what is wrong with me, or has it already, by the grace of God, been dealt with?" Thinking like this can prove to be quite the conundrum.

In Isaiah 3:8-9 God says: "Jerusalem staggers, Judah is falling; their words and deeds are against the Lord, defying his glorious presence. The look on their faces testifies against them; they parade their sin like Sodom; and they do not hide it."

The destruction of the city of Sodom occurred because the wickedness in that city was so great God could take it no longer. The poor were being marginalized and sexual immorality was paraded in such an evil way the people of the town were preparing themselves to have sex with complete strangers, even though they knew God's law! Now that is some heavy parading of sin! Let me ask this: What would your reaction be if I told you I thought we, by living in shame, were parading our sin before God just like the city of Sodom? I'm not saying that we are, but if we are going to attempt to be real and call sin evil, what should the punishment be for us Christians? We somehow find the nerve to stand before God and sing, "What a Wonderful Maker," all the while believing that He did not fearfully and wonderfully make us! I am talking about unbelief.

What should the punishment be in comparison to that of the city that decided God's commandments were not worth obeying and that they were going to trust what made them feel good more than the God who created their emotions? I understand that God destroyed the city of Sodom because of its selfishness, wickedness and perversion of sex and I am not saying we should be comparing ourselves to such a city. However, I sometimes wonder if God would be justified in destroying the church because of the way we have chosen to view ourselves (as the problem). We are shaming ourselves after being told who we are because of the greatest creation, that was followed by the greatest sacrifice, which gave us the greatest gift. Simply put, God has given us an identity that is free of bondage and can allow no shame to cover our faces and we have believed that we are not who God says we are. We have turned away from God and screamed, "I am still the problem!"

Believing we are something other than what God has said we are is shame. Simply put, believing we are the problem after God's own Son has cleansed us from the sin that once filled us is not accepting the truth that we have been made clean by the blood of Christ. Living in shame is, in fact, not acknowledging that Christ's blood has been poured over us, washing us clean from this seemingly powerful lie. Is it possible, if we are bringing shame upon ourselves, that it is because we do not understand God's grace?

For some, turning away from our identity and living under

the control of shame comes simply from hearing the words fat, ugly, stupid and any variation thereof. For others, these words cannot even begin to explain the way in which we feel about ourselves since we believe we are dirty beyond recognition and that we must fix or clean ourselves. "Letting it go" is the closest pseudo-outlet we have found to freedom. Since the memories will not fade, we lock ourselves up in the belief we will have to live our lives in the pain that comes from being deeply wounded by someone (whom we can barely look at in the face).

For many of us, forgiveness appears out of the question. Most of us would prefer to sit back and be a victim for the rest of our lives. We dump our pain onto anyone who will listen with the hope they will tell us, "You're not dirty," when in all honesty it doesn't matter what anyone else says. The belief that "once you're dirty, you're always dirty" has infected our belief system all the way to our vision of our truest selves. Some of us like to keep secrets. "What will people think of me if I tell them who I really am?" We have faked our way through life and people have believed we are who we say we are. However, all of this might not matter if we knew God has been calling our name ever since we first started sewing our own fig leaves, hiding and then blaming. "Rod, what are you doing?" God says, "Be honest with Me. Let me tell you who you really are. I love you. I think that you are radiant. Look to Me. It is time to stop hiding." The choice is ours.

6

Glory

So how does it work when we finally decide to be open and
honest with God? What does God do? What happens to us? Let's
look at three people from God's word and see just how everything
turned out for them when they were laid bare before God.

> In the year that King Uzziah died, I saw the LORD seated
> on a throne, high and exalted and the train of his robe filled
> the temple. Above him were seraphs, each with six wings:
> With two wings they covered their faces, with two they cov-
> ered their feet and with two they were flying. And they were
> calling to one another: 'Holy, holy, holy is the LORD Al-
> mighty; the whole earth is full of his glory.' At the sound of
> their voices the doorposts and thresholds shook and the tem-
> ple was filled with smoke. 'Woe to me!' I cried. 'I am ruined!
> For I am a man of unclean lips and I live among a people of
> unclean lips and my eyes have seen the King, the LORD Al-
> mighty.' Then one of the seraphs flew to me with a live coal
> in his hand, which he had taken with tongs from the altar.
> With it he touched my mouth and said, 'See, this has touched
> your lips; your guilt is taken away and your sin atoned for.'
> Then I heard the voice of the LORD saying, 'Whom shall I
> send? And who will go for us?' And I said, 'Here am I. Send
> me!' (Is 6:1-8).

Isaiah acknowledged his state before God two times in this
passage. The first time that Isaiah saw the LORD he knew he was

unclean and without giving shame any time to manifest itself in him, Isaiah confessed his belief of being ruined before God. Isaiah was real in the presence of God and was washed clean. The second time Isaiah was faced with the opportunity to be real was when God asked, "Whom shall I send?" It would have been very easy for Isaiah to say, "No way, I'm not even worthy to be here." It would have been easy for Isaiah to hide from God since shame constantly tells us, even after we have been made right with God, that we are still the problem. But Isaiah held his ground and said, "Here am I. Send me!" Had Isaiah not believed he was who God said he was, he would have fallen back into the exact same place where he started, except this time Isaiah would have been bound by the cycle of shame. For Isaiah, being real with God allowed him to confess the shameful state in which he was living before God Almighty and receive a new identity that had no shame in God's presence. Isaiah looked to the LORD and became clean.

A second individual to be real before God was Hannah.

> There was a certain man from Ramathaim, a Zuphite from the hill country of Ephraim.... He had two wives; one was called Hannah and the other Peninnah. Peninnah had children, but Hannah had none. Year after year this man went up from his town to worship and sacrifice to the LORD Almighty at Shiloh, where Hophni and Phinehas, the two sons of Eli, were priests of the LORD. Whenever the day came for Elkanah to sacrifice, he would give portions of meat to his wife Peninnah and to all her sons and daughters. But to Hannah he gave a double portion because he loved her and the LORD had closed her womb. And because the LORD had closed her womb, her rival kept provoking her in order to irritate her. This went on year after year. Whenever Hannah went up to the house of the LORD, her rival provoked her till she wept and would not eat. Elkanah her husband would say to her, "Hannah, why are you weeping? Why don't you eat? Why are you downhearted? Don't I mean more to you than ten sons?" Once when they had finished eating and drinking in Shiloh, Hannah stood up. Now Eli the priest was sitting on a chair by the doorpost of the LORD's temple. In bitterness of soul Hannah wept much and prayed to the LORD. And she made a

vow, saying, "O LORD Almighty, if you will only look upon your servant's misery and remember me and not forget your servant but give her a son, then I will give him to the LORD for all the days of his life and no razor will ever be used on his head." As she kept on praying to the LORD, Eli observed her mouth. Hannah was praying in her heart and her lips were moving but her voice was not heard. Eli thought she was drunk and said to her, "How long will you keep on getting drunk? Get rid of your wine." "Not so, my lord," Hannah replied, "'I am a woman who is deeply troubled. I have not been drinking wine or beer; I was pouring out my soul to the LORD. Do not take your servant for a wicked woman; I have been praying here out of my great anguish and grief." Eli answered, "Go in peace and may the God of Israel grant you what you have asked of him." She said, "May your servant find favor in your eyes." Then she went her way and ate something and her face was no longer downcast. Early the next morning they arose and worshiped before the LORD and then went back to their home at Ramah. Elkanah lay with Hannah his wife and the LORD remembered her. So in the course of time Hannah conceived and gave birth to a son. She named him Samuel, saying, "Because I asked the LORD for him" (1 Sam 1:1-20).

Some find difficulty in this story because they cannot understand how someone like Hannah can pray in bitterness of her soul to God and have God answer her request. In reality, the issue for Hannah was not whether or not she was bitter before God. The issue was whether or not she was going to be real or fake.

Many Christians find it easy to be fake with God every day. We go to church on Sunday morning and mouth pious hymns, all the while believing God did not fearfully and wonderfully make us. Not so Hannah. The moment shame came against her, telling her she was the problem because she could not conceive children, she took her thoughts captive and sent them directly to the only true God. But Hannah was bitter! So what? In the deepest part of her soul, where she was hurting beyond explanation, she decided to be laid bare before God and at that very moment God rescued her from every fragment of shame that had been covering her face.

Notice this shame brought upon Hannah did not come with flares and flashing light bulbs. Peninnah, Elkanah's other wife, spoke lies to Hannah and told her she was the problem. And if that was not enough, this even came from her own husband, Elkanah! Remember? "Hannah, why are you weeping? Why don't you eat? Why are you downhearted?" Hannah was probably wondering why in the world her very own "knight in shining armor" wasn't protecting her from all of the fiery darts being flung her way. A seemingly more innocent but most devastating attack came from Elkanah who asked her to look to him for peace and assurance! "Don't I mean more to you than ten sons?" Talk about a guilt trip! Yet in the midst of all of this deceptive torment, Hannah endured and stood her ground, keeping her eyes fixed on the only one who could rescue her from the shame. Hannah knew that the only way she was ever going to experience freedom was if she fixed her eyes on God, the author and perfecter of her faith. Being real with God was where Hannah found freedom from shame. Freedom from shame is glory, otherwise known as luminosity. Hannah looked to the LORD and became radiant.

Finally, there is King David. For many of us, David brings to mind the young boy who slayed a giant Goliath, winning land and freedom for his people from the invading Philistines. Some of us can almost hear David telling Goliath he will strike him down and cut off his head. Others see David as a sinner who not only had a horrible affair with Uriah's wife, Bathsheba, but also got 70,000 men killed when he did not heed the prophet's warning and sent out a census numbering his fighting men. But most of us remember King David in the words of Acts 13:22:

> After removing Saul, [God] made David their king. He testified concerning him: "I have found David son of Jesse a man after my own heart; he will do everything I want him to do."

That is probably the most awesome compliment God ever gave someone in the Bible, aside from Jesus, His own Son. God chose David as a man after His own heart because God knew

Remembering a Forgotten Grace

David would "do everything I want him to do."

David didn't see God as someone to be taken lightly. In Psalm 145:20 he wrote, "The LORD watches over all who love Him, but all the wicked He will destroy." David didn't define who he thought God was and place Him in a box, like many of us do. David saw God as the only true God who created the universe. The only true God worthy to be praised.

Did David mess up? Well, if one considers letting one's eyes wander away from the Lord and onto another man's wife so that one decides to kill that man, then yes, David messed up. But think about this: when David was confronted with His sin, the Bible says he confessed by saying, "I have sinned against the Lord" (2 Sam 12:13a). David did not make any desperate attempts to cover his sin in front of Nathan, the prophet who rebuked him. It would have been simple for David to claim it was Uriah's own fault he was dead. He could have hid from God and denied the truth that he was being laid bare and his sin was being exposed. He also could have blamed a countless others for what he knew was his own sin. However, for some reason none of us can see King David blaming Bathsheba for bathing outside on a hot summer day, nor blaming Uriah for agreeing to go to the front lines of battle. All we see is David, a man after God's own heart, being real and allowing God to take away his shame. After David confesses his sin Nathan says, "The LORD has taken away your sin" (2 Sam 12:13b).

Of course there were consequences for David's sin. His son that he had with Bathsheba died. This was a horrible experience for David, but the shame that gripped him was taken away when he looked to the Lord. David was a man after God's own heart and when he looked to the Lord he became radiant with no shame over his face. How do I know he became radiant? Some people, at this point, might be wondering why "looking to the Lord" is not getting rid of shame. I know this because David was the one who coined the idea in the first place; just check out Psalms 34:5.

7

Illumination

"I sought the LORD and he answered me; he delivered me from all my fears. Those who look to him are radiant; their faces are never covered with shame" (Ps. 34:4-5).

Sometimes I wonder what it means to be radiant and not to have my face covered with shame. A different translation of this verse says, "Those who look to him for help will be radiant with joy; no shadow of shame will darken their faces" *(New Living Translation)*. Now I was raised believing Christ's death on the cross and resurrection from the dead freed us from guilt and shame for all time. However, reading this verse makes me wonder if the possibility still stands that I could have some form of shame dwelling inside of me, or at least a shadow on my face so that radiance could not be seen. This is a scary thought.

The Bible says in Exodus that after Moses had looked to the Lord he placed a veil over his face so that the people of Israel would not stare at him in all his radiance:

> When Moses finished speaking to them, he put a veil over his face. But whenever he entered the LORD's presence to speak with him, he removed the veil until he came out. And when he came out and told the Israelites what he had been commanded, they saw that his face was radiant. Then Moses would put the veil back over his face until he went in to

Remembering a Forgotten Grace

speak with the LORD (Ex 34:33-35).

What does this mean that Moses looked to the Lord and became radiant? Paul tells us, "We are not like Moses, who would put a veil over his face to keep the Israelites from gazing at it while the radiance was fading away" (2 Co 3:13). This radiance faded, which means that to have it fade from one's face means it had to be visible in the first place. Radiance, for Moses, was so evident a veil was required to keep others from staring. Significantly, Moses' face was not covered in shame. Then, in order for his face to be radiant, Moses had to be covered in something else. This is where we understand why the definition of Glory must possess luminous qualities. Paul explains it thus:

> Now if the ministry that brought death, which was engraved in letters on stone, came with glory, so that the Israelites could not look steadily at the face of Moses because of its glory, fading though it was, will not the ministry of the Spirit be even more glorious? If the ministry that condemns men is glorious, how much more glorious is the ministry that brings righteousness! For what was glorious has no glory now in comparison with the surpassing glory. And if what was fading away came with glory, how much greater is the glory of that which lasts! Therefore, since we have such a hope, we are very bold (2 Co 3:7-12).

The next verse is critical in dealing with the question posed earlier. Is there a possibility that I could have some form of shame dwelling inside of me, or at least clouding my face, so that radiance could not be seen? The simple answer is found in 2 Corinthians 3:13a: "We are not like Moses." The Glory of God, which brings to us jaw-dropping radiance, places an illuminated and unfading reflection of Him, the only Luminous God, upon us! Our faces are never covered in shame!

Recently I came across the following analogy on the back of the Dave Crowder Band's booklet from their CD, *Illuminate* (2003): The sun is luminous—and the single source of light for us every day. However, the moon is not luminous. Moonlight, although fascinating, proves to be a shabby rendition of that which is truly brilliant. The moon appears at night to help us see, but in order for people to understand true light they must look to the sun. The moon points people to the sun because it reflects the sun's luminosity, but by itself the moon possesses no light. The moon has looked to the sun and become radiant. The moon is not luminous, although it has become illuminated.

As long as the sun is shining, so shines the moon. The moon's radiance is not dependent upon its own ability to create light. If it were, the moon would have a problem because it cannot create light and would therefore be clouded in shame. In looking to the sun, the moon remains radiant. Even if it tried to create its own light, or glory, the moon would continue to shine because, although it cannot create its own light, the moon will continue to reflect glory from the sun, not from itself. So, we are as the illuminated moon and God is like the luminous sun. Nothing we can do will take this radiance away from us! Our faces are never covered in shame.

Many of us grow up never consciously learning about shame, yet in the back of our minds we have the nagging question, "What is wrong with me?" The problem is not that our faces are covered in shame, because as believers our faces are never covered in shame, but because we believe that who we are is what is wrong and we live our lives with this as the basis of our of belief system.

I remember the first time that I began to discover shame in my life. I was in the third grade and I was apologizing for everything. If I thought that I had said the wrong thing to my parents, I apologized. If I felt I had disobeyed them I would apologize. I even remember apologizing by saying, "I'm sorry if I ..." basically did anything. One time my father pulled me aside and told me to stop apologizing or else I was going to get a spanking. One can imagine the very next words out of my mouth. "I'm sorry for saying I'm sorry." Shame.

The issue for me as a third grader was not in deciding whether or not I should have actually said I was sorry for whatever I might have done, but that I believed I was really sorry. In other words, I was a sorry person. Instead of experiencing guilt, I was creating for myself a belief system that was beginning to define who I believed I was. I was apologizing, not for what I had done, but for the person that I believed I had become.

Shame takes root in our lives when we are young. Young men no longer desire to play with the doctor or male nurse action figures like their parents and grandparents did. They want the extra-ripped, extra-strong, extra-manly, super-human action figures. Usually these toys are so extreme in their proportions that if they were life-sized they would be too large to fit into a house. We are told that unless we lift enough weights, take enough drugs or wear the right clothes, we will never be real men. But what we find ourselves striving to be is not real at all. The Incredible Hulk, James Bond and Superman are not authentic people, but for some reason we strive to become like these fantasized macho images in order to escape the shame which is telling us we will never be great. We believe we are disgraces and, unless we do something to fix ourselves, we will never amount to anything worthy of recognition.

Adam and Eve fell for the same trick.

8

Hungry

Jesus said, 'Have the people sit down.' There was plenty of grass in that place and the men sat down, about five thousand of them. Jesus then took the loaves, gave thanks and distributed to those who were seated as much as they wanted. He did the same with the fish (Jn 6:10-11).

When I read about Jesus' life and ministry on this earth, no matter who He was with, no one ever went hungry. Location never mattered, time never mattered; when Jesus was around there was enough to eat. Think of all those people who stood around with their families thinking, "How on earth am I going to feed my children? Jesus sure is a great guy, but I'm starting to get hungry."

As the crowd begins to become restless, Jesus says to the disciples, who are feeling the anxiety of 5,000 hungry men, "Where shall we buy bread for these people to eat?" The disciples realize, as Philip says, "Eight months' wages would not buy enough bread for each one to have a bite." At this point, you can feel the stress rising as the disciples bring forward a young boy with five barley loaves and two small fish. "Here is all that we have Jesus, but how far will this go among so many?"

This is the moment when Jesus is at His best. We, like the disciples, have reached into our pockets and discovered our wealth is not enough. All we might earn cannot hold a candle to what Jesus is about to do. This is when we hear those powerful words. "Have the people sit down."

Maybe God has been telling you to sit down, stop what you are doing and listen. What if God knew the shame you face every day is more than you can handle? What if God knew that even though you try, over and over, to rid yourself of all of this pain, it never leaves? What if God knew that what you are carrying is too heavy? Imagine yourself standing in a crowd, shamed with the feelings of aloneness, feelings you have had since you first met Him. What would Jesus say?

Can you see Jesus looking through the crowd, seeing you stand in frustration and self-hate, knowing nothing you can do will ever be enough? You are out of food, nourishment, sustenance and provisions. You have been run dry. You have nothing and feel as though you have become nothing. In that moment of shame, when worthlessness is attempting to root itself into the deepest part of your soul, can you see Jesus looking past all of the other faces until His face is focused on yours and then saying to the disciples, "Have the people sit down"? It is time to eat. Ridding your life of shame is not about what you need to do, or say, or be; it is about realizing where you are already.

These 5,000 people were fed because they were exactly where they needed to be, sitting at the feet of Jesus, listening to His every word. Can you hear His voice? Are you ready to sit down and eat with your King? Let's take a look at someone who discovered the amazing reality of eating at his king's table:

> So Judah went into captivity, away from her land. This is the number of the people Nebuchadnezzar carried into exile: in the seventh year, 3,023 Jews; in Nebuchadnezzar's 18th year, 832 people from Jerusalem; in his 23rd year, 745 Jews taken into exile by Nebuzaradan the commander of the imperial guard. There were 4,600 people in all (Jer 52:27b-30).

What would it have been like to have a kingdom, like Jehoiachin, the king of Judah? Imagine how important that must have made him feel? Then what would it have been like to see the entire kingdom fall into King Nebuchadnezzar and Babylonian captivity? One day Jehoiachin is sitting on his throne enjoying life, the next he is laying on the floor of his cell hoping the guards will not notice he hasn't been beaten yet. On one hand, I have no idea what Jehoiachin went through, but on the other I know that he and I are exactly the same.

Here I sit behind bars that, just like Adam and Eve, I know I have put into place. It is as though I have fallen and there is no possible way I could ever get up. As I look out past my cell I am reminded of all the places I wanted to go but cannot, because I have been taken captive by that which I have feared the most: the Babylonians. Those who wish to define me are constraining me to the place in which I've never wanted to dwell, my own prison. I have become shamed before my enemy and as I lay bare before others, I realize that I have been humbled before my God. I have nothing left to defend. I desire to try and cover my own nakedness, but I know that sewing will do no good for my clothes are filthy. I seek to hide, but there is nothing in my cell to shade me from the truth that others are looking at me for who I really am, scared and wounded. I want to blame, but no one is listening. Everyone is staring at me as I make myself look even more foolish by proudly stating that it is not my fault I have landed in this cell. They guffaw as I attempt to tell them I am indeed king. What I say holds no weight, for we all know I am not a king. I am a prisoner and the only one who can free me from my prison is a King who cares more about me than I do for myself.

> In his 37th year of Jehoiachin's exile, Evil-Merodach became king of Babylon and released Jehoiachin from prison on the 25th day of the twelfth month. He spoke kindly to him and gave him a seat of honor higher than those of the other kings who were with him in Babylon. So Jehoiachin put aside his prison clothes and ate regularly at the king's table. Day by day the king of Babylon gave Jehoiachin a regular allowance

as long as he lived, till the day of his death (Jer 52:31-34).

How wonderful it must have been for Jehoiachin to walk free. One moment he is in the depths of despair, the next he is dressed regally, eating at the king's table. What an experience! What do you suppose was the defining moment was for Jehoiachin? Why was he released from this painful state of torment in "the year Evil-Merodach became king"?

Jehoiachin was not just simply freed from prison to fend for himself, but he was given a new wardrobe and told to sit at the new king's very own table. With this in mind, let me ask a few questions. Who was Jehoiachin's king when his freedom was being trampled on by the Babylonians? He was. Who was Jehoiachin's king before he was set free from his literal prison of despair? He was. Who was Jehoiachin's king before he took off his disgusting prison garments to exchange them for brand-new royal linens? He was. This story points out that at the moment when we are convinced we are in charge of our lives, we put ourselves in a place where we must either turn to a new king, who will set us free from our current state of being, or we believe we are deserving of this prison in which we find ourselves living.

The problem with shame is that once we have reached the bottom, we believe we are supposed to stay there and live with the hand that we have been dealt. We have sewn fig leaves, made many excuses and tried to hide multiple times, but we have failed. As we find ourselves sitting in silence with this pain and fear of being rejected once again by others, or even worse, ourselves; we discover that we are staring in the face of hope. Our new challenge is to look past the prison walls and see that the one who put us here is dead. King Nebuchadnezzar, our captor and our past circumstances, are no longer in control of who we are. We need to sit down and listen.

Can you hear a new King calling your name? However long He has been whispering to you does not matter. Today is the day, your royal wardrobe is waiting and the feast is almost prepared.

So what do we do? Our families may think that we are dead or at least out of hope, but we keep hearing Him say, "Lazarus, Come out!" Our friends are frightened by the storm, but we keep clinging to the word, "Come," and we step out onto the waves. We have lived our lives convinced there is something better than the way we have been living and thinking. "Rod, come be real with me. Let me tell you who you really are. I love you. Wear my clothes. Look to me. It is time to stop hiding. Let's eat." And we find ourselves once again at a crisis moment, a moment that will continually present itself to us. Here we are again. So what do we do? The choice is ours. Can you hear your King?

Ultimately, there are two different types of shame: legitimate and illegitimate. Both are lies. However, legitimate shame comes from sin whereas illegitimate shame comes after our sin and legitimate shame have been taken away. Simply put, legitimate shame comes before forgiveness and illegitimate shame comes after we have been forgiven. When Adam and Eve sinned and became covered in shame, sin was the problem. Now, just as Adam and Eve thought that they were the problems, so do we.

We are born into a world that is fallen. Although we are created in the image of God, when given the opportunity where we can either choose God or choose sin, we tend to choose sin. We are shamed because of the decisions we make, but this is legitimate shame. Usually, we attempt to cover this cloud of shame over our faces by sewing a fig leaf, which means we strive to cover our legitimate shame with anything that makes us feel good about ourselves, or at least deceive others into believing we are doing fine. Or else we hide or we blame. Most of the time, we can see the evidence of sewing when we come to church on Sunday mornings.

Imagine an entire room filled with hurting people. Each person is wishing to find some form of relief from the judgment which they are under every day. Everyone sits in fear, wondering if their crisis moment will come today. They hope for that moment which will deliver them from all of their problems, but it does not come. Is this the church? Instead, the very place that was intended to bring restoration and healing brings judgment and condemnation. For some reason, people find it difficult to look at each other with gracious eyes, so to escape shame, we sew more and more fig leaves until we find ourselves swimming in a pool of conformity and phony faces. We pretend we are not clouded with shame.

Soon the room of people is smaller. Only the best sewers, those who feel they have mastered their craft, remain. Those who announce they are sick and tired of pretending to be something they are not, revealing what they believe to be their true selves, which is shamed and weak, have been kicked out and forbidden to return to this so-called holy space. We claim boldly we must "expel the immoral brother or sister" yet we live in fear of being expelled by those whom we pretend to trust should our fig leaves be removed unexpectedly.

Is this the church? Some of us see through our own feeble attempts to be acceptable and since we cannot win the battle in our own minds by sewing, we hide—because we fear if our true selves are revealed, we would be told to leave because the Bible says we are the problem. We tell ourselves the church is only a group of judgmental hypocrites who want nothing more than to dissect our lives with Bible verses, explaining what awful people we have become.

We do not want to go to church because we know that when it comes to sewing, we cannot keep our fig leaves on. We have tried, but ultimately we find ourselves being honest and in so doing, we become a scapegoat for all of the good sewers to point their fingers at and say, "Someday he will be like us. Someday he will reach our level." So we stay away, hiding and hoping no one comes knocking on our door. We are tired of playing the religiosity game and do not even want to be seen because our fig leaves never stay in place and we're not good at being phony. We hide if the sewing did not work or if we have previously been rejected and marginalized by the "good sewers." Sometimes we can hide for extremely long periods of time and sometimes we cannot. Either way, we almost always learn how to blame.

We feel like we have been marginalized or pushed out of the one place we had initially come seeking restoration. We realized once we arrived, we were forced either to be fake or honest and if we were honest we became the prostitute at whom everyone was aiming their stones, ready to punish. We told ourselves that although we initially had come into the church wounded, the sewers have wounded us more. Therefore it was their fault that we were being ostracized and condemned by others.

We call ourselves oppressed and make it known we have not been accepted in the past and now must be heard. We believe the time to speak out is now, yet dare not say the only reason we are where we are is because we were not able to sew strong enough fig leaves and pretend to be spiritual like the others. We dare not say that had we been good sewers, we would have stayed with the others and climbed the ladder of fame and false glory. But we were not accepted. We were honest, or so we believe, and it is their fault we have not been accepted nor heard. It is their fault that we cannot be who we believe that we are.

So we blame. We blame others for our wounds and we do not forgive. These people, these sewers, are our enemies. We dare not pray for them, because they will not accept who we are. We have sewn fig leaves because we are covered in either legitimate or illegitimate shame and the fig leaves have fallen apart. We have hidden from others in the fear of what they might think of us. We have blamed many people, calling them sewers who are phony and intolerant, because of the shame that is clouding our faces. We do

Remembering a Forgotten Grace

not want to be the problem and yet we will not fall on our faces and admit we cannot be all that we know deep down we must be. We are not sick and tired of being sick and tired and until we are–and are willing to sit down, stop trying to be heard and listen, we will never know what life is like when living under the grace of Jesus Christ. Will we be naked before God, or will we continue in our own feeble attempts to cover our own shame?

I would like to clarify that this book has not been designed to set anyone free from shame, fear, guilt, or anything else, for that matter. The Bible is the only living written word and it is capable, through the Holy Spirit, of correcting our minds and training us to live under the righteousness of God (2 Tm 3:16). But, if you, like me, have found yourself sick and tired of being sick and tired, then I challenge you to drop all of your presuppositions about yourself and others and seek the face of God who will not turn us away but rather welcomes us into a reality that, deep down, we have always known existed. This reality is where we find ourselves made in the image of God Almighty, restored to His likeness in true righteousness and holiness and knowing His truth that never fails to continually set us free. This is where our journey takes a sharp and deliberate turn.

Part Two

Remembering a Forgotten Grace

9

Body

Once upon a time there was a boy who wanted to be loved by everyone. He lived in a large town with many people and wanted to be loved by them all. Each day the boy would spend his time running around the town attempting to prove himself acceptable to every person he saw.

Usually, the boy would run to the clothing store where people always wore the latest and most popular clothes and there try on many different new styles of clothing. He would spend lots of money on hats, gloves, pants, shirts and any new or popular article of clothing that happened to be on the market that day. The boy would always purchase something before he left and the people at the clothing store would always continue going about their business.

Next, the boy would go to the place where everyone ate all the new flavors of ice cream. He would order many different flavors and combinations of ice cream in many different shapes and sizes. He usually ate all of his ice cream and was always the first person to try the newest flavors. The people at the ice cream store would happily give him ice cream and then they would always continue going about their business.

After eating the ice cream, the boy would usually go to the

places where everyone sang the newest and prettiest songs. There he would sing the loudest of anyone, always making sure he was heard above the rest of the singers. Every time a new musical instrument was brought to the place the boy would be the first to purchase the instrument. Everyone would sit and watch him play it and then they would go about their business.

This happened every day. The boy rushed and rushed around the town trying to fit in and be loved by everyone. For some reason he thought the more he knew and the more he was able to do, wear, eat or sing, the more he would be loved by everyone in his town. Little did the boy know that as he was spending all of his time running around by himself trying to be loved, everyone else was going about their own business.

The boy knew everyone's name. They all wore name tags. The people at the clothing store wore name tags so that other people would know that they were clothing dealers. The ice cream people wore name tags so that everyone would know from whom to buy ice cream. The singers all wore name tags so they could know who each other was. It is very difficult to keep harmony and sing at the same volume when people do not know each other's names. The problem was that they did not know the boy's name and he did not know his own.

The boy would spend his time trying to be like the clothing salespeople, but he could only purchase clothes from them. He did not sell clothes, because that was not who he was. The boy spent his time eating many different flavors of ice cream, but he could not make the ice cream for he was not an ice cream maker. The boy would sing louder than any of the musicians, but it did no good because no one could hear him. He was always outside on the street looking in through the window wishing a new instrument were up for sale so that he would be allowed inside to make his purchase; otherwise he could not go in. He was not a musician. In fact, he did not know who he was.

As the boy walked home one day from his grueling task of trying to be loved by everyone, he noticed a small grasshopper sitting in the grass. "I wish I could be that grasshopper," the boy said as he crushed its body into the dirt with his popular new shoe. He said, "It had no problems, no worries and it didn't have to try and be like anyone else." As the boy continued his walk home he thought if he could go back to that moment when he had killed the grasshopper he would have let it live, because the grasshopper knew who it was and he did not know who he was. The boy concluded that if one does not know his name he will live as though he has been crushed, because he has been, by people who did not know their own names. He will crush others, because that is all that he will know how to do; crush others because he has been crushed. "What is my name?" the boy thought as he continued walking home. "I wonder if I will ever be acceptable to others?" he mused. The boy stepped on three more grasshoppers, two ants and a dragonfly as he walked home. He wanted to be loved by everyone, but in all reality he could love no one.

Day in and day out the boy rushed around town attempting to be loved by others and loving no one. Then on his way home he crushed others because he had been crushed and continued living his life in fear of never knowing his own name.

This is the performance-based life.

I wonder if we are like this boy? Obviously, all of us have been wounded. We all have "stuff" in our past. Sometimes I wonder if the problem is not so much that we have been wounded, but that we do not know how to love each other through our wounds. Instead we crush each other. Paul writes that, "anyone who eats and drinks without recognizing the body of the Lord eats and drinks judgment on himself" (1 Cor 11:29).

Growing up and hearing that passage of scripture, I always thought I needed to sit in my pew and confess every sin I had ever committed before stepping forward and receiving the elements;

otherwise I was going to be condemned to hell. This was especially true when I read the previous verse which says, "Whoever eats the bread or drinks the cup of the Lord in an unworthy manner will be guilty of sinning against the body and blood of the Lord" (v. 27). Today, this is not what I believe Paul was saying when he was speaking about receiving the body of the Lord in an unworthy manner. I think that he was talking about us. If we truly are the body of Christ, like the Bible says we are, are we bringing judgment upon ourselves because we do not receive each other with good hearts?

Imagine a room filled with all different kinds of people who have come together for a celebration – but not any normal celebration. This is a get-down, jump-around, scream-at-the-top-of-your-lungs party. The food is delicious. The decorations are extravagant. The people are dressed beautifully and the guest of honor has arrived. But there is one small problem: everyone there hates each other. In fact, the people who are there cannot even stand to be in the same room with one another. There is so much grumbling and complaining one would think they were at an annual church board meeting – not a party. Oops, did I say that?

My point is that we, the church of Jesus Christ, do not receive each other well and therefore are bringing judgment upon ourselves. Paul told the Corinthians that was why many of them were sick and had fallen asleep – or died. Is it possible, as Christians, to bring so much shame and guilt upon each other that we are making ourselves sick and possibly killing each other? I think so. I'm sure many of us can think of multiple times when we have been shamed by another believer, manipulated to believe we are disgraceful. We can remember when we were not only accused of having done something bad, but gossip had been spread to make us appear to be the problem. Our brothers and sisters have shamed us and it is wrong.

But haven't we done the same thing? Haven't we accused and

blamed in our desperate attempts to cover our own shame? We sewed elaborate fig leaves that did not cover our nakedness well enough and our brothers and sisters who ridiculed us and told us that we could never be good enough called us out shamefully. Yet now we stand around the church door and do the same thing. "He smokes." "She's a lesbian." "I know what they do every Friday night." "If the other members only knew! I guess it's not gossip if I'm telling the truth." We point our fingers and smile or frown, depending on what everyone else is doing and make ourselves appear "holier than thou." We are the best. We have become the best sewers, the best hiders and by far the best blamers. Are people only grasshoppers to us? Is it not enough that we spend all of our time trying to make ourselves acceptable, but that we must now crush each other with our words and actions? Do we not wait for each other? Must our own needs always be met first? Can we stop condemning each other and be judged by the Lord?

"When we are judged by the Lord, we are being disciplined so that we will not be condemned with the world. So then, my brothers, when you come together to eat, wait for each other" (1 Cor 11:32-33).

Community is the gate to overcoming individual shame. True community does not demand others become like us, but rather loves people unconditionally, not demanding results. In the end, unconditional love is the only thing that will bring about healing. Any other attempts will only leave us sewing, hiding and blaming and no matter how good we are at those three tasks we will never know how to love and therefore be loved. "We love because He first loved us" (1 Jn 4:19). Is it possible that Christ may want to love others through us first, ridding their lives of shame and guilt, so that they may ultimately be able to love others? What would happen if we were that authentic and loved people just because they were created by God?

What would happen if unconditional love were loosed on this earth, or even just in the church? If Christ could truly love unconditionally and He gave us the power to love others unconditionally, what does that mean? Can we truly change the world one life at a time? If loving individuals can truly change the world, then what is stopping us from bringing this Gospel to the nations? Do we think the people need to meet some kind of prerequisite in order to hear the Good News? Do we think others need to change their lifestyle before they can change their life?

Why are we so selfish? Are we so busy pretending we ourselves do not struggle with life, sin or irrational feelings and trying to convince others that we are acceptable? Are we so busy that we do not take the time to be authentic people? Do we think God made us so that we, individually, will not struggle through life? Do we think that if we try hard enough, or fake it long enough, that we will reach some type of utopian state of sanctification where everyone is strong in their faith and full of tranquility? What is it going to take for us to be honest with each other?

10

Striving

It is strange how so many Christians believe on Judgment Day all of our sins will flash before our eyes. No wonder so many dread that day for fear they will have to face all of their impurities and failings. Of course, everyone having to see their own sins will be distracting enough so people will not notice the transgressions of others. Unless, of course, everybody has to stand in a really long line while God goes through each person's life, one at a time. That would be one shameful experience. I'm sure glad we only act like that now, attempting to place each other's sins on the big screen, while we are still on Earth. What would happen if we were actually honest with each other and ourselves? Could we then be honest with God?

What would church be like if everyone had to wear their sins around their necks. Imagine walking into a room filled with beautiful chairs and smiling people. Obviously, the room is full of grace. Looking around you see everyone has various signs hanging from around their necks. Each person has a cardboard sign with an inscription, plus two holes punched in the upper corners. A string connects the two holes making it possible for them to hang the signs around their necks so they can be easily read. What is odd, however, is what has been written on the signs. Each sign has

Remembering a Forgotten Grace

only one word on it. And each word is a SIN. For example, one man bears the word LUST. Only that word is allowed and he is not able to explain why this word is on his chest. One could assume he is addicted to pornography, or that one day, when he was 16, he had a bad thought. Another man has ADULTERY boldly written on his sign. No one knows if he actually committed adultery or if he just did it in his heart. As Jesus said, "If any man looks at a woman lustfully, he has committed adultery with her in his heart" (Mt 5:28). One woman has MURDER written on one of her signs, but no one knows if she actually killed someone or has she just hated her neighbor in her heart and as Jesus said, murdered him? (Mt 5:22). The point of this would be that no one would be able to distinguish their own sin as any better or worse than another's. People would all look at just one word at a time and odds are, everyone would have every sin hanging across their chests.

Don't you think people would like such a church because they wouldn't have to pretend to be something they are not, nor wade through half the worship songs, repenting over and over again, before feeling good enough about themselves to sing praise to God. Such a service would be a lot more about grace and a lot less about not sinning. Children would be able to come to church and not feel as though they must strive to reach some sort of "holy level" in order to be acceptable to the rest of the church.

Paul writes, "It is for freedom that Christ has set us free. Stand firm then and do not let yourselves be burdened again by a yoke of slavery." He continues, "Mark my words! I, Paul, tell you that if you let yourselves be circumcised, Christ will be of no value to you at all" (Gal 5:1-22). But today's church appears to have let itself be circumcised by a list of rules and regulations which bring on an excess of shame and guilt. Paul asked the Galatians, who were becoming immersed in such a problem, "What has happened to your joy?" (Gal 4:15a). I ask the same question. Have we become so caught up in making ourselves acceptable and causing others to attempt to make themselves acceptable that we have lost our joy? Are we crushing each other because we have been crushed? Are we condemning each other because we have been condemned?

What if the answer to shame lies in the ability to love others unconditionally and in so doing, being able to rest in the grace and shadow of the cross of our Lord and Savior Jesus Christ? Paul said it this way: "May I never boast except in the cross of our Lord Jesus Christ, through which the world has been crucified to me and I to the world. Neither circumcision nor uncircumcision means anything; what counts is a new creation" (Gal 6:14-15). What if we could love each other as we have been loved? I think this kind of love would do so much more than rid our lives of shame. This kind of love just might change the world. As a matter of fact, I think He already did.

I remember a Saturday night college worship service while I was in Amarillo, Texas. The service was called "Seven," and as I listened I began to appreciate the speaker's take on some passages in Philippians. A combination of Philippians 1:6 and 2:12 says: "being confident of this, that He who began a good work in you will carry it on to completion until the day of Christ Jesus.... Continue to work out your salvation with fear and trembling."

The Greek word for "work" in Philippians 1:6, "ergo," means "to toil." Paul explains that it is God who began toiling in us when we were given salvation and that He will continue toiling in us until the day that Christ Jesus returns. This is the process of sanctification every believer experiences and that every believer will see come to completion on the day that Jesus is revealed.

In Philippians 2:12, Paul uses a different word for work. *Katergazomai* means "to distribute the work (or toil) thereof." So Paul is saying that it is God alone who toils in us, so we can stop trying, striving and pushing to reach a point of holiness that only the finished work of the cross can obtain. God's toiling in us is producing a greater sanctification than the holiness so many Christians strive for today–"Christian perfection." We are stuck in a "Toilet Bowl Christianity" where we do nothing but strive, grit our teeth, judge the way others are pushing and produce nothing but rubbish. It is time to realize that God alone, through His Son Jesus Christ and His indwelling Holy Spirit, "is our righteousness, holiness [sanctification] and redemption. Therefore, as it is written: 'Let him who boasts boast in the Lord'" (1 Cor 1:30b-31).

I think Adam and Eve began boasting about who they were, or at least who they thought they could be if they had more knowledge. We do that too. Our educational system says we must attain certain degrees and prestige in order to be heard and our media says we must look or act a certain way in order to be watched. Does this seem like some weak attempt to make ourselves into gods?

During college I found myself helping out with a weekend Christian rock concert. Some extremely popular Christian bands were there and everyone seemed excited to see these important faces. I had volunteered and was placed on the prayer team. Basically, the prayer team would walk around and talk to people who were attending the different shows, or sit in the prayer tent and wait for people to come in to pray or talk.

One evening a young man came into the prayer tent asking if we could pray with him. He said he had a hard time getting the nerve to make his way over to us because there was just something about coming to a prayer tent that made him uncomfortable. I could definitely understand what he was talking about, because many times I had felt that others would always stare or think, "I wonder what is wrong with him?" as I would make my way to the altar some Sunday mornings at church. Nevertheless, this young man fought through the shame and ended up standing before us, the assumed "mighty prayers," beside the water cooler under the tent. He informed us he had recently incurred a loss in his family and just wanted to pray with someone. We prayed with him and everything seemed to be looking up when I discovered he was a huge fan of one of the recording artists at the concert.

This recording artist was one of the biggest names in Christian music and I had an all-access pass. I was excited. I decided to sneak this young man to the front of the autograph line, past the security fence and right in front of the main stage for the show. Was he excited! He jumped around like I had never seen anyone jump before. And there he was–pretty much all by himself–six feet from the stage. He loved every minute of it. Shortly after the concert a guest speaker came to speak to everyone about the Bible and then about an organization that supports hungry children. The young man asked if he could take a beach ball with him as he and almost everyone else left to go buy t-shirts, wristbands and CDs while the preacher was speaking. The sermon was good, but since no one was there to hear it I wondered how much we, as a Christian community, attempt to idolize one another and in so doing become like gods?

What bothered me most was not what happened after the concert that day, it was what happened a few hours before while we were sitting in the prayer tent relaxing and talking to people. Within a matter of minutes it became clear that all the autograph tents were full so our tent was going to have to be used as an autograph signing area for this same, extremely popular Christian musician. I helped the people set up tables and chairs, creating a barricade so that the musician would not be overwhelmed with fans. Everyone stood in an extremely long single-file line and I noticed that, as everyone filed through to get their autograph, the prayer tent had turned into a concession stand of more t-shirts, wristbands, stickers and CDs.

Don't get me wrong. This is not a huge legalistic attempt to say preachers are better than singers and that a prayer tent should always stay a prayer tent, or that children should never run in the sanctuary. However, I do wonder how many young teenagers, like the young man I met, stood in line for extended periods of time waiting to get autographs which they thought would bring them some sense of peace, or release, or love. How many teenagers think these preachers and musicians have no problems and that if they can only get close enough to them, they will somehow feel better about themselves or discover what life is like when one doesn't struggle.

I've been there and am there every day, depending on what I hear the preacher say on Sunday morning, because for some reason I have exalted others above the human race, telling myself if I could only be like them life would be easy. Why do I feel that I need to be like them? Am I, once again, the problem, or have I just created another idol? Why do I always choose shame over glory? Let's take another look at C.S. Lewis' quote: "Either Glory means to me fame, or it means luminosity. As for the first, since to be famous means to be better known than other people [or God Himself], the desire for fame appears to me as a competitive passion and therefore of hell rather than heaven." He continues: "As for the second, who wishes to become a kind of living electric light bulb?" (Lewis 2001:36).

Since the beginning of creation, all people want glory. In the beginning, they were given glory. Adam and Eve had glory, the glory of the Lord. In fact, God's glory was all around them. But for one reason or another, we all desire our own and I'm beginning to think this is because we want fame. 1 Corinthians 13:12 says, "Now we see but a poor reflection as in a mirror; then we shall see face to face. Now I know in part; then I shall know fully, even as I am fully known." But we want to know now, we want to not sin now, we want to know ourselves like we are known, we want to not be on a process, we want it all now; we want to be like God. Maybe we desire fame, instead of grace. What if the answer to our search for glory has already been given, but we have not yet looked in the right place? What if grace is the answer?

11

Church

When I told a friend I was writing a book dealing with shame and unconditional grace, I was warned not to go too far off the deep end and allow the pendulum to swing to another extreme. To me it was obvious how far the church has fallen into a performance- or works-based system of religion, but the thought of going off the deep end with grace had me perplexed.

What would happen if grace were preached from today's pulpits as it is truly meant to be preached? What if we didn't have to worry about how we were going to stop sinning but instead this all-empowering presence of God made our lives no longer about not sinning? What if our lives were meant for a greater purpose than to spend our time listening to monotonous sermons about how we can somehow be free from sin by not doing it anymore and then trying our very best not to sin, somehow proving ourselves acceptable to God and the rest of the church? Either that, or we could all become really good at sewing, hiding and blaming.

It seems when the church decided we would tell our children that not sinning was the key to success in the Christian life, we forgot about grace. The answer was not to invent a plan or write a book which would provide people with steps to help them overcome sin. The answer was grace and for some reason we forgot about it. We forgot about grace.

I believe that we are believing a lie. Personally, I want to know the truth. As Jesus said, "You will know the truth and the truth will set you free" (Jn 8:32) and trust me, I want to be free from all of this strivingly-produced "crapology."

So why do we spend all of our time trying to define what is sin and what is not? Do we want to know if certain deeds such as masturbation, smoking or drinking are right or wrong so that we will know how to feel when we commit them? Isn't it the Holy Spirit's job to convict us of sin? If it is, then why are we so afraid to talk about what seem to be tough moral issues such as these? I think the answer is exactly that, we are afraid. Many of our lives are being run by guilt and shame, or by fear of both.

If I were to ask any group of people what they would do not to have guilt, fear or shame in their lives, they would probably say, "We would do anything." If they were anything like the rest of us, they have probably tried almost everything. What if life were not about not sinning – which includes living in guilt, shame or fear? What if, instead, life were about being covered by the blood of Christ and being taken on a journey? This journey would be a process, a life-long experience, where people slowly begin to understand themselves and, at the same time, they are understood. Gradually, everyone begins to know themselves as they are fully known. What if, instead of striving to reach sinless perfection, people were placed on a road where they would see God face to face and fully understand grace? They were not there yet, but that it was okay? And what if faith, hope and love were with them and, as they began to understand more, they began to love others with the same love that they were seeing in the heart of God?

What if life were not about not sinning? Oh, what a life that would be. A life that is so consumed by the grace of God that when other people ask, "What is different about her?" the answer would be, "She realizes now she no longer needs to prove herself a saint and she has stopped trying. All of who she is can be accredited to the grace of God."

I can imagine one of the first people who actually understood this concept. She was a prostitute and, in my opinion, she was at the house of God, or at least right outside the doors. Her story is in the gospel of John:

> But Jesus went to the Mount of Olives. At dawn he appeared again in the temple courts, where all the people gathered around him and he sat down to teach them. The teachers of the law and the Pharisees brought in a woman caught in adultery. They made her stand before the group and said to Jesus, 'Teacher, this woman was caught in the act of adultery. In the Law Moses commanded us to stone such women. Now what do you say?' They were using this question as a trap, in order to have a basis for accusing him. But Jesus bent down and started to write on the ground with his finger. When they kept on questioning him, he straightened up and said to them, 'If any one of you is without sin, let him be the first to throw a stone at her.' Again he stooped down and wrote on the ground. At this, those who heard began to go away one at a time, the older ones first, until only Jesus was left, with the woman still standing there. Jesus straightened up and asked her, 'Woman, where are they? Has no one condemned you?' 'No one, sir,' she said. 'Then neither do I condemn you.' Jesus declared. 'Go now and leave your life of sin.' (8: 1-11).

In this critical moment when Jesus confronts those who might call themselves "the church," one might find it different to note that He does not, not even once, mention this woman's sin to the people standing around her. Jesus does not say, "I know this woman is a prostitute and is living a life of sin; but come on, we all have good hearts, can we not just love her even though we hate her sin?" No, in fact Jesus does the exact opposite. He says, "He who is without sin among you, let him throw a stone at her first" (8:7).

Jesus makes life extremely simple at this moment in time. He pretty much says if you are going to think about anybody's sin, it had better be your own. Everyone needs to put his stones down now. However, Jesus doesn't stop there. He does confront the

Remembering a Forgotten Grace

woman, but it is only to show her that when Christ intervenes "there is therefore now no condemnation" (Rm 8:1a). When He finally does address this woman's sin, Jesus speaks to her as a new creation, one that cannot be judged by anyone but Him, even though she has just been caught in adultery just moments earlier. The woman did not even have the right to condemn herself. She could only "go and sin no more."

The painful question begins to haunt us: "But what happens if, or better yet, when the woman sins again?" What happens when she gets dragged to the streets a second or a third time, because she has sinned again? What will she do when everyone has picked up their stones one last time? Maybe this is the last time. I think the better question is, "What will Jesus do?" I can imagine Jesus doing the exact same thing again. He would say, "He who is without sin among you, let him throw a stone at her," and then He would begin writing in the sand as all the rocks fall to the ground, including her own. Then Jesus would say, after revealing once again there is no condemnation for those who are in Him, "Go and sin no more."

A new hope must have arisen for that woman when she heard those words, because maybe she understood them in a way that made her life not about not sinning, but about never being condemned. On top of that, once Christ had become a part of her life she would always be new. No matter what she had done, was doing (condemning herself), or would do, she could always "go and sin no more."

I can't help wonder what Jesus meant when He told her to leave her life of sin. Some might think that He meant stop sinning completely, but that is not what I think. I think Jesus told her to leave her lifestyle of sin, to leave the things bringing condemnation upon her—such as fear, guilt and shame—because I do not think this woman went back home and began to worry whether she would ever again commit adultery. For this woman, Jesus had injected Himself into her life, so leaving her ways of sin was about so much more than striving not to be a prostitute. Her life was no longer about living in secrecy and fear of the Pharisees, whom she knew on a first-name basis. She was no longer shamed and no longer guilty. Even if she had attempted to convince Jesus of her guilt, He would have only said, "Who condemns you?" and she knew the answer to that question. This woman's life had been changed and it was no longer about sin or fear of what sin might do to her. Her life was about being the person who she was in that moment, a person who mattered to Jesus Christ, the very Son of God.

Christ changes our lives. He not only changes our focus and our attitude, Jesus changes what we are about. Once we enter into that precious, all-empowering, unconditional relationship with Him, our lives are no longer about finding convenient ways not to get stoned. Our lives become about Him. Slowly, our feeble claims to acceptance are shattered by a brilliance that must be perceived as glory from Jesus, our Luminous God. That is the beauty of grace. "I sought the Lord and He answered me; he delivered me from all my fears. Those who look to him are radiant; their faces are never covered with shame" (Ps 34:4-5).

Sometimes I wish I could have been that woman, because maybe I would have been able to understand grace better than I do. Part of me does not want to commit a sin as bad as hers, which shows how poor an understanding of grace I actually have. I feel, maybe like you, that I have faked longer than I wanted to, hid better than I wanted to and blamed and thrown stones harder and more accurately than I ever wanted to. When will the church realize we have been trying to drown each other while we are all swimming in a pool of grace? What is it going to take for us to stop playing Holy Spirit and let God convict of sin? When will we turn to God for justice and the body of Christ for grace? We are the church, Christ's body. We need to be Him.

Return to us, O God Almighty! Look down from heaven and see! Watch over this vine, the root your right hand has planted, the son you have raised up for yourself. Your vine is cut down, it is burned with fire; at your rebuke your people perish. Let your hand rest on the man at your right hand, the son of man you have raised up for yourself. Then we will not turn away from you; revive us and we will call on your name. Restore us, O Lord God Almighty; make your face shine upon us, that we may be saved (Ps 80:14-19).

12

Excellence

When I think about Adam and Eve in the Garden of Eden, after they had sinned, I see them as being in their first church service. I mean they had spent all of their time attempting to cover themselves. They were ashamed, so they hid and then blamed each other so that God would not look upon their flesh and so they would not look upon each other's nakedness. However, I think it is funny because God did not ask either one of them who started the whole ordeal. He doesn't ask if the serpent had a hand in it. He doesn't ask if Eve ate the fruit first. He said, "Who told you that you were naked?" (Gen 3:11).

I would ask you the same question. With no attempts to cover your nakedness, without hiding and with no blaming allowed, I ask you: Who told you that you were naked? Why do we see ourselves as the problem? Who told us that who we are is unacceptable to be laid bare before each other and our holy God?

I spent a summer in China where I learned that relationships cannot produce change or bring about anything good without unconditional love and grace. To come into contact with a person who has never heard the Gospel and expect to say words to them that will change their life is completely absurd to those who are involved in world missions. Without a genuine relationship based on the love and grace of God through Jesus, no words will be effective, but with these relationships the world would probably begin to change, and fast.

As a church we talk a lot about being excellent and doing ministry in an excellent way. We use the verse, "Be wise about what is good and innocent about what is evil. The God of peace will soon crush Satan under your feet" (Rom 16:19a-20). Many times we want nothing more than for the Devil to be crushed. We think if that happens we will somehow be able to lead sinless lives and so we push to become good at what we think is good and innocent of what we think is evil.

But what is good and how can we be excellent at whatever it is? I contend that Jesus Christ, incarnated as God in the flesh is good, as God is good. For us to be excellent at being good we must become Christ. Maybe, instead of saying our ministry must be excellent or that we must always focus on trying not to sin, we can say that in order for anyone to become Christ-like, they must immerse themselves in Christ's very own body, the true church, which is God's gift to the world.

When we become the body of Christ in true form, life no longer is about special formulae or antics that will cause us to be strong individuals. Rather, life is about revealing the grace of God to others in the same way it was first revealed to humankind: no stones, no guilt, no condemnation, no shame. Creation has been waiting eagerly for the manifestation of the children of God (Rom 8:19). So here we are. The choice now is, are we going to be the body of Christ or are we going to spend our lives trying to be excellent at something we have defined as good? We can be excellent at what is truly good. We can be excellent at being Christ. "For by grace you have been saved through faith and this is not of yourselves; it is a gift of God, not of works, lest anyone should boast. For we are His workmanship, created in Christ Jesus for good works, which God prepared beforehand that we should walk in them" (Eph 2:8-10).

The Pharisees were always about being excellent, especially when it came to being clean. A person had to be clean before they could enter the temple to worship, both inwardly and outwardly. The Pharisees even complained to Jesus about how his disciples were unclean because they did not wash their hands before eating. Basically, Jesus' followers were being called dirty – and not by just anyone. The highest and most religious of all sought them out and called them on breaking the tradition of commandments. The disciples did not wash their hands properly and now they were being shamed for it. Here is how the story goes:

> Then some Pharisees and teachers of the law came to Jesus from Jerusalem and asked. "Why do your disciples break the tradition of the elders? They don't wash their hands before they eat!" Jesus replied, "And why do you break the command of God for the sake of your tradition? For God said, 'Honor your father and mother,' and 'Anyone who curses his father or mother must be put to death.' But you say that if a man says to his father or mother, 'Whatever help you might otherwise have received from me is a gift devoted to God,' he is not to 'honor his father' with it. Thus you nullify the word of God for the sake of your tradition. You hypocrites! Isaiah was right when he prophesied about you: 'These people honor Me with their lips, but their hearts are far from Me. They worship Me in vain; their teachings are but rules taught by men'" (Mt 15:1-9).

Jesus basically tells the Pharisees that His disciples are not the ones breaking tradition, but rather they are by thinking of themselves as holy and more righteous than others because of what they were doing, keeping a man-made law. The Pharisees believed being close to God meant preaching the law and honoring Him with their lips. They taught doctrines that were nothing more than rules and regulations that kept others motivated by guilt and shame, causing people to believe that they were screwed up.

Jesus said, "Hear and understand. Not what goes into the mouth defiles a man, but what comes out of the mouth, this de-

Remembering a Forgotten Grace

files a man" (Mt 15:10-11). People listened to the Pharisees preach condemnation in their doctrine of commandments day and night. What makes this story "funny" is the thought that the only things coming out of anyone's mouth were rules and regulations from the Pharisees, the ones who were causing all of the performance-based living. The woman who was about to be stoned said nothing to defend herself and the disciples did not argue about not washing their hands. These people neither condemned nor condoned their actions, because in that moment they were with Jesus. Nothing else mattered.

Jesus continued on after dealing with the Pharisees and said to His disciples: "Every plant which my heavenly Father has not planted will be uprooted. Let them alone. They are blind leaders of the blind. And if the blind leads the blind, both will fall into a ditch (Mt 15:13-14).

How many ditches do you suppose the church has fallen into? Sometimes I think we dig them ourselves. I know one thing for sure, we never see them coming. What if we, instead of attempting to fix ourselves, could, "Fix our eyes on Jesus, the author and perfecter of our faith, who for the joy set before Him endured the cross, scorning its shame" (Heb 12:2)? Have the Pharisees told us that we are naked?

Sometimes I wonder why we have so many self-help books regarding team building and working well with others. Maybe we only write these books because there has never been a good example. I remember hearing a story, whether true or not, about a guy who wrote a book on raising children. It was a good read and a best seller. The problem was that he was not married and had never raised children in his life. I wonder how many of these self-help books which we have today are products of never having to actually live those principles. Either that, or nobody wants to admit they do not actually know. Maybe it is the fact that people everywhere seem to have an extremely difficult time being vulnerable with each other. Those who do not have a problem sharing themselves with others we call dysfunctional and tell them to guard themselves and their hearts from being hurt.

What if my weaknesses were not weaknesses, but rather greater opportunities for others to show me unconditional love and grace? If my weaknesses were actually weaknesses, then maybe people could say that I have a lot of Christian maturation or growing to do. What if instead my weaknesses were opportunities for a team, community or body to invest themselves in me? Maybe instead of praying to God every night to make me strong, I could exclaim like Paul that God's grace is truly sufficient for me no matter what and that "When I am weak, than I am [truly] strong" (2 Cor 12:10).

To me, a community is a place where people, anyone, can go and be accepted and loved without having to do anything. To me, unconditional acceptance means people do not have to change to be a member of a group but that being loved and shown grace is the initiation. Church should not be about making sure people stop doing something, but instead start doing everything. Which means we must put down our stones and ask those who stand beside us, "Who condemns you?" and when they say, "No one," bring them into that communal presence where ministry is best accomplished, in genuine, unconditional, grace-filled relationships. The church has more potential than any other group of people in history. We stand on grace, which is our rock. We have not built on the sand.

Maybe our problem is not that we have earnestly been trying to convey what we believe about life and death, but rather that we have not come to the table with all we have to offer. We have not come with grace and, consequently, we have not come with truth. So here we stand, in a circle, staring at each other from all sides. We have been wounded in the past and so we grip our stones tightly. It is in this moment we must say, "Today is the day of salvation," and put down our stones. We are the body of Christ.

Remembering a Forgotten Grace

Let us be the body of Christ.

I cannot wait for the day when we all meet together in heaven for the first time. It will truly be amazing to see the radiance of God's glory reflecting on each of our faces. I think the most beautiful experience will be to see a community gliding smoothly and graciously, as if they are one body. Sometimes I do not think I can wait for that day. Then I am encouraged, because today I can give others a glimpse of how that day will be, when everything is new and all of the grace is unconditional, a day when there will be no guilt, no fear and no shame. So for this moment, this day of salvation, I am a member of the body of Christ and today, that is who I want to be.

13

Bob

One night I talked with a man named Bob who was 71 years old and had been a Christian for seven months. Bob was letting me stay in his house, for free, for an entire summer as I completed an internship for my bachelor's degree. That particular night I was telling Bob about my trip to China and how in ministry, building relationships was much more effective than preaching from the street corners and, in the long run, even better. Bob agreed with me as I continued to talk about how in America we always have the tendency to want to sell things and in order to do that we must advertise. We Americans try hard to sell Christianity without the relationship aspect but when I was in China all I did was build loving, unconditional relationships with people.

Bob told me he thought that was wild, which gave me enough nerve to continue on my soapbox. I pointed out how we constantly tell people Jesus will make them happy but that just is not true, for Christians can be sad in life. At this point Bob stopped me, "Oh, Rod, you don't know. He sure did make me happy." I sat in awe as this man, like Stephen, began to unravel before my eyes the secret to the happiness on which I, all this time, had been blaming health-and-wealth theology. Bob said, "I'm not rich, but I'm content." He went on to explain that in the middle, between happy and sad, was content; sure it had its ups and downs, but no matter what happened, being content was steadfast to him. Bob was content and God was getting all of the glory.

Just when I thought that I had learned enough for one evening Bob looked at me and said, "Do you think you have a purpose? You don't have a purpose." Then as I was almost in utter disbelief he pointed up and said, "He has a purpose." In essence, Bob was telling me he was content because he was not his own. He had an unconditional relationship with Jesus Christ. But that was not all. With a clever looking grin on his face Bob said, "You know, there is a price for staying at my place. You're not getting off for free."

I thought, "I hope he doesn't ask for more than $200." "What's that?" I said, returning the smile. "Every Christmas you have to send me a card, just a note telling me how you're doing." "Deal," I said. Right then Bob's daughter telephoned wondering how he was doing and I began thinking what it means to be in a genuine, unconditional relationship with someone. I owed Bob more than I could pay and all he wanted was to know me more – and in the process showed me what church was truly all about.

We think we owe God more than we could ever pay Him, but actually we owe Him nothing. This may be difficult to understand, but the truth is Jesus paid every debt we could ever possibly incur and because of that gift our lives are not about striving not to sin or living good lives free of shame, fear and guilt. In fact, Jesus Christ's death and life were so influential upon His Father that God does not operate upon whether or not we believe that we are the problem. We live in an age of grace and just like Bob, God wants nothing more than to know us as He already knows us, holy and acceptable to Him, because of Him. What if the church today could allow the same grace that penetrated the throne room of God, allowing Him to forget our sins as far as the east is from the west, to penetrate our hearts and minds and show us what church is all about? How would our lives be different?

14

Unity

Psalm 133 is a beautiful song of the ascents. It is the second to last of a series of 15 songs and it takes place as David is approaching the end of his journey. His striving and toiling are complete. It is almost as if David has finished his journey, at least his pilgrimage to the temple and similarly to Paul, has finished the race. Reading Psalm 133, one might notice the significance of what he says in this moment. David does not write a song with a chorus that exclaims, "Try hard and one can reach his goals," or, "No matter your journey, do not give up. Anyone can achieve her dreams if she is willing to fight for them."

Those thoughts are not in David's mind and heart as he approaches the one place he has traveled so far and struggled so hard to reach. As David approaches the gates to the city where he will soon worship God, he is not focused on what it takes to overcome. David, a man after God's own heart, after all of his toiling and striving to reach the temple, is not focused on what he has achieved. Past deeds and future sins hold nothing against the moment David is preparing to experience. The hardships of yesterday, which he has written about in Psalm 132 have passed and as David is beginning to enter this climactic place of worship, he has one thing on his mind, the body of believers, or as we might say it,

Remembering a Forgotten Grace

the church. He writes:

> How good and pleasant it is when brothers live together in
> unity! It is like precious oil poured on the head, running
> down on the beard, running down Aaron's beard, down upon
> the collar of his robes. It is as if the dew of Hermon were
> falling on Mount Zion. For there the Lord bestows His bless-
> ing, even life forevermore (Ps 133).

If the holy Trinity is such a mystery that its graceful luminosity in unity beckons us to try and understand the God of the universe, I wonder what a free-moving body of believers in a world
that is a mess of chaos beckons? If God's Son, becoming human
and living in perfect unity with His Father, was powerful enough
to rise from the dead and is still impacting people thousands of
years later, I wonder what His current Body, in a world seeking
deliverance from performance-based condemnation, can give.

What would happen if the church, just like Jesus, could look
past the sins of others and begin to bring people into that holy
place where nothing else matters but the grace of God through
Jesus? "Today is the day of salvation" (2 Cor 6:2). Let today be the
day when we come together in unity, having stopped sewing and
stopped hiding, having put down our stones and say, "Hi, my
name is _____ and I am a radiant child of God."

Let today be that day when no matter who anyone else says
they are, upon entering our presence we respond by knowing their
name and saying, "Neither do I condemn you," and in so doing,
letting them know what the church and unconditional love are all
about. Let us be remembered as a people of grace, a people who
loved first, loved second and then loved third. "How good and
pleasant it is when brothers dwell together in unity.... For there
the LORD bestows His blessing, even life forevermore" (Ps 133:1,3).
There is something about the grace of God that brings life and in
the case of the body of Christ, life forevermore. "I sought the
LORD and He answered me; He delivered me from all my fears.
Those who look to Him are radiant; their faces are never covered
with shame" (Ps. 34:4-5).

15

Titles

I grew up in a family that was constantly in and out of recovery centers dealing with family issues. I remember sitting in a chair, with my feet dangling back and forth, too short to touch the ground, looking around an Alcoholics Anonymous meeting as people told their stories of dysfunction, fear, shame, guilt, addiction, rejection and other horrible circumstances which had caused them to separate themselves from the other Pharisees around them. One would think that a seven-year-old would have a hard time understanding the reality of what was actually occurring in those meetings. But I did understand. For me, reality was honesty and without honesty everything was a counterfeit of some lifestyle that had been seen either on television or preached about Sunday morning from the pulpit. I understood those meetings extremely well.

I understood what it was like to be placed in a room of people who appreciated each other and for people to be honest with themselves and not always attempt to provide answers for everyone else's problems in the room. I realized that answers, many times, were defense mechanisms designed to keep others from focusing on our blemishes. I knew what it was like to be accepted for who I was and not where I was or what I was thinking, doing or feeling. To say, "I am wounded," was to agree with a community that said, "We are all wounded," and no one was perfect. Although we were all hurting, bleeding and many times felt like we were dying, we were all being mended back together through the fellowship we experienced every week in a circle of chairs.

At first we lived in fear of what others would think of us when we were laid bare before this seemingly weak and broken community (which we had strived so hard to avoid) because we believed we were so strong. Slowly, we became authentic and nothing was going to stop us from healing. We had found freedom in the truth that it did not matter how we introduced ourselves. "Hi, my name is Rod and I'm a _____." Back then, for me it was "child of an alcoholic." Today it has become so much more. But none of that is important because no matter what I say in that moment, I will always be greeted with the same phrase, "Hi Rod." Rod is who I am and that will never change until the day in which I am given a new name, an unmarked name, by Jesus Christ Himself.

In Alcoholics Anonymous I learned who I truly am is not defined by the many titles which society wants to place upon my head. I will always be Rod. Some people can accept that and some just cannot. That does not matter as much to me anymore, because I know there truly are people who have learned to look past the scars which I have accumulated over the past years of my life and who can see my heart. Those people are my family. Is this the body of Christ?

16

Perfection

I have read books that have attempted to convey the importance of grace while simultaneously talking about the importance of not sinning. It was as if the writers were saying life needs to be all about being made right with Christ, covered by His blood and immersed into an existence where deeds do not matter in regards to how God sees us, whether or not He was pleased; then they said, "So now stop sinning." The question for me was motivation. I wondered if finding a motivation not to sin that would override our desire to sin had been the churches' focus since the fall?

Various ones have claimed that grace changes our motivation so that we will not want to sin and the more that we become immersed in God's grace, the more of a conqueror we will become in order that we live holy lives. The problem here is that humans have always had a tendency, just like Adam and Eve, to attempt to cover shame on our own. So what happens when we sin? And we will sin. More than likely, we will once again have a greater temptation, because this does not stop once we sin; it is scheming both before and after so we will be convinced we are the problem. The greater temptation will be to see ourselves as not immersed in the grace of God or even the Holy Spirit as we think we ought to or should be. Our striving and motivation for perfection is shat-

Remembering a Forgotten Grace

tered when we sin and once again, in our minds, we become the problem and are convinced we need to fix ourselves.

Because of this I ask why, when writing or talking about grace, must we always find ourselves traveling back to a place where we are striving not to sin so that we can be pleasing to God and others? Can we not see this is the same as returning to a slab of concrete that used to be a prison but had its barred walls destroyed, and living there as if we are trapped by our own surroundings? It is one thing to attempt to do pleasing things, knowing that without grace these works are dirty and disgusting, but it is another matter striving to become pleasing to God and others by what we do or don't do. There is a difference between knowing that who we are is acceptable and pleasing to God because of His Son and living in a performance-based religion that stops nothing short of perfection, teaching people to act as if they are perfect, while at the same time thinking and feeling as if they are the problems.

17

Grace

I struggled with this section, especially the ending, because I wondered if I needed to explain in a different way how grace and sin compare and contrast. I knew I had basically said, with a sort of wrecking-ball theology, that grace destroys the power of sin in the lives of those who have a relationship with Jesus. I also knew that I had written how Christians need to unite together under this grace, without condemning spirits and become Christ's body to the world, representing the grace which Jesus had come to bring. However, I struggled because I knew we have always felt as though we needed to have everything fit into our fallen and rational brains. Therefore, an open-ended book did not seem to make much sense; but neither did grace.

The great part about grace is that although it will never fit perfectly into our heads and our emotions will never be able to comprehend nor apprehend such a presence, grace will always fit perfectly into our lives. We need grace. We do not understand grace, but we need it. We need grace like Moses who, trembling before his own people wanting to kill him and afraid of the pursuing Egyptians, lifted up his staff and watched the sea part before his eyes. We need grace like Noah who, although ridiculed, rejected and shamed by the rest of the world, managed to build a

Remembering a Forgotten Grace

boat like one he had never seen before. We need grace like Esther who, in fear of her life went before her husband and king, restoring salvation to her people. Our world understands the all-empowering presence of grace even less than we do and because it has not acknowledged the fit of grace into its life, we need to be grace. For that, we must be the body of Christ.

This is where shame ends. In a body so graceful it moves like water, being the problem is not an option. Fig leaves are not needed and hiding is out of the question because everyone has dropped their stones and instead of looking condemningly into the other's eyes, they instead ask, "Who condemns you?"

The world is in awe of a community such as this. "It is almost as if they are one person," I can hear someone saying, who has been rejected by family and friends. "Those people love you just because you're you," others might add, who had previously been kicked out of church because they thought they were gay. Shame is never experienced in a place where people experience grace. Jesus taught us how to love and we must love as He loved.

Many of us have been to the place where we found ourselves tired of covering our shame with poorly sewn fig leaves. We have found ourselves hiding and wanting nothing more than the freedom to be who we are and still be loved. We are sick of blaming and being blamed. The rocks hurt too bad to keep going. Yet, in the middle of this turmoil, some of us have given up on striving to be perfect and pretending as if we are not hurting. Some of us, in the midst of our pain, have looked up and found grace, the grace to be ourselves, to make mistakes and to be in a process to be finished on the day when Christ Jesus is revealed. Now we know that as the body of Christ, we can be that grace to people who are no different than us.

"Hi my name is Rod and I'm a _____." What is said next is up to us. We can send this person down a tunnel of performance-based legalism, thinking somehow not sinning is the answer, or we can be what we are called to be, the body of Christ, the church, a place of unconditional grace. This is where shame loses power because when people are with Jesus, they never go hungry and nothing else matters because there is therefore now no condemnation.

That said, my challenge to the church is this: Find grace – in its pure, most powerful and rawest form. Find grace unaltered by your strivings to become perfect. Look in the places you have never looked and find grace. Look past your deeds, whether seemingly good or bad, and find grace injecting itself into your every move. Find grace in the God-man standing in a circle of people with a prostitute who has done nothing to defend herself or make herself right. Find grace in Jesus and then be it to everyone else. We are the body of Christ; we need to be the body of Christ.

Remembering a Forgotten Grace

Part Three

The Bride of Christ

18

Newness

One time I felt as if God told me to love Him like a girl. Don't get me wrong. I did not think God was telling me I was supposed to love Him like I would love a girl, but rather as if I were a bride and He was my groom. I realize what I am writing may seem to contradict the current, human-warrior masculinity movement, but trust me, it doesn't. There is a temptation in our church to think of humans as something they are not. For we are not gods, we are humans, mere mortals. When faced with difficult situations, we are always presented with a choice and many times we make the wrong one. Humans cannot be God. Nonetheless, we do try. We strive to reach a place of individuality where we are strong enough to live lives on our own. This is a place where, we believe, others will come to us for help and where we will need no one. This is a temptation for humans and this temptation was confronted in me one Sunday morning while I was asking God to what He was calling me.

I remember the setting. The church was called The River. The pastor was out of town at a conference and another man was bringing the word of God that day. I remember being frustrated because the first words of his presentation were "Three Require- ments to Hear God's Voice." Now that bothered me because I had just finished reading Donald Miller's *Searching for God Knows What* (2004) and I was thoroughly convinced a defect in the world was not all of the problems that people are attempting to prove humans have, but that we are inventing more and more issues and then trying to deal with them as if we are gods, or at least wanting to be more important than others.

However, when the three requirements in order to hear God's voice turned out to be that I had to have a relationship with Jesus, be surrendered to Him and be reading His word, I was not quite as upset as I thought I would be. I did disagree with some of the sermon, mainly because God spoke to King Nebuchadnezzar and others like him in past, but I could understand where this preacher was coming from, so I stopped getting mad and decided to listen.

It was a good sermon and I recall his telling how God affirmed him in his time of "hearing God's voice." He was being called to start a new church in the neighborhood, because he thought he heard God tell him to and God's voice was affirmed through his experience and people giving him different verses in the Bible. He then asked us to take time to ask God what He was calling us to.

As I tried to do just that, a girl came to the front of the church to play the piano. I thought about how churches always try to make emotional experiences out of everything and that it would probably be better if she wasn't playing songs while I was attempting to pray. So I preached myself a little sermon on the topic, in my head of course. Eventually I began to focus, but then the guy next to me started moving around and I was distracted. "He is having a hard time praying," I thought, "I wonder how long this thing will last. The guy said ten minutes. I guess that it's going to be awhile." So I started to pray again.

I spent some time just wanting Jesus to edify me in my spirit, or whatever it is He does in our spirits. Then I looked up and saw the question on the screen we were supposed to be asking: "God, what are You calling me to?" "What a weird and performance-based question," I mused to myself. In my mind I could imagine people leaving church and saying things like, "God is calling me to stop sinning all together," or "God is calling me to tell people to stop sinning all together." That thought bothered me because there really are people in the church who believe that not sinning or telling people not to sin is their calling and there are others who just tell people that, because not sinning is what they have heard preached their whole lives.

I wondered why we live in this performance-based Christianity, telling each other that what we do defines who we are. I thought of that line in *Batman Begins* (2005) where Batman tells his love the exact same thing before he jumps off of the roof and spreads his electrically hardened wings: "It's not who I am on the inside, it's what I do that defines me." I then thought, "Our church is truly going down the wrong road." Finally I stopped thinking and asked: "God what are you calling me to?"

That moment began something in me which I am only beginning to understand. What I feel God said challenged me and changed my life. Don't get me wrong, it was hard to swallow, especially at first, but when God began to reveal His truth to me about His purposes for my life I realized what He was calling me to was worth my time, my effort and my transformation. Here is what God told me and before deciding I'm truly crazy, please take the time to allow His truth to permeate your heart and mind and then decide. God said, "Rod, I'm calling you to love Me like a girl." I thought, "What in the world does that mean?"

I had lived my life, striving to be a real man, or at least what I thought a real man was. Some days I would feel better than others and some days I would feel completely horrible. I mean, I wanted to be a man, but I didn't want to be a girly man. To have God telling me, "Rod, I'm calling you to love Me like a girl," was throwing me for a loop. Needless to say, I asked God what He meant. Then it hit me.

Remembering a Forgotten Grace

I remember thinking that yes, God is my Father and I am His son and God does love me like His son, but He also loves me like I'm a girl. I realized, in that moment, in probably a more literal way than ever before, that I, along with my surrounding community, was the bride of Christ. I was Jesus' bride and He was my Groom. "Oh boy," I thought, "Where is this going?"

The next day I was talking with the pastor's wife. I had been staying with this family for about a month and I felt a little weird telling her what God had recently revealed to me. "God told me that He is calling me to love Him like a girl," I said. Then I went on to explain how I had realized that I was the bride of Christ, but that was all that I could say. I didn't know anything further than what God had told me, but I knew that this was going somewhere.

I was partially surprised because I was expecting her to say something like, "That's different Rod," or "That's interesting. I've never heard of God speaking to a male like that before," but she did not react the way I expected. The next day she handed me a note card with a verse written on it. Jeremiah 2:2: "I remember the devotion of your youth, how as a bride you loved Me and followed Me through the desert, through a land not sown." Then she recommended that I read an excerpt out of a series called, *Breaking Free* (2000), by Beth Moore. The devotion was touching on what it meant to be the bride of Christ and I was interested. As I read and contemplated the verse she had given to me I began to realize something profound.

A bride is always new. She is dressed in white and pure. It is almost as if in that moment of giving oneself to another, a bride has made herself ready. She has made preparations and is excited about embarking on a new adventure together with her groom. Revelation 19:7-8 says, "Let us rejoice and be glad and give Him glory! For the wedding of the Lamb has come and His bride has made herself ready. Fine linen, bright and clean, was given her to wear." I can imagine a bride on her wedding day knowing God has made her for this moment. God has kept her pure, not because she has never made mistakes, but because with Jesus all things are always new. I can see the newness in the place of vows, where two people have come together ready to experience each others' hearts fully, for the first time.

This is grace, because we are by no means perfectly pure people. A wedding ceremony is about grace. Understanding this, we can know that for us to begin to experience ourselves as brides before Jesus, our groom, we must immerse all that we know ourselves to be into this grace and then begin to realize what actually happens to two people when they become one together. There is no distinguishing one from the other.

I could understand this "no more distinguishing" a little because my sister Kelly had just married a wonderful man, Jason. Before they were married, even while they were engaged, Kelly was still my sister and she always will be, but something strange happened after her beautiful wedding day. I no longer could think of Kelly as Kelly. Every time that I thought of my sister the thought was always, Jason and Kelly. This bothered me at first because Kelly was my sister, but then I realized that she was more than just my sister now. My sister was the bride of Jason. Kelly was no different from him in the sense that these two had become one. There was no more distinguishing. Jason and Kelly possessed all of each other.

This is grace. Jason and Kelly are not one because they never made mistakes in their lives and came to each other on their wedding day flawless. They are one because God's grace enables people to be continually new. That is why forever my sister Kelly is always the bride of Jason. She loves him; she will go anywhere with him – even through the desert.

A friend who worked with me on a street ministry team that he and another man started in Michigan once told me a story. The

Remembering a Forgotten Grace

ministry has street teams, mentors, in-home Bible studies and prayer partners, but it quickly advanced and found new avenues to reach the lost of the inner city. We were discussing healing one day and he completely blew my mind, expanding my understanding of the grace of God, especially in marriage.

Once a mentor of his was speaking at a church in New York City when a prostitute came to the church while he was preaching. That day she received Christ as her Lord and Savior and was also delivered from prostitution and the spiritual implications that come along with living in sin against one's body. Some time later a young man in the church became interested in her and decided to befriend her. They began to talk but she was wary of bringing pain into his life because of her past. He didn't seem to care and eventually asked her if she would date him. They discussed how she felt, but no matter what she said to him about her past, the young man responded by telling her how much he loved her, all of her. Some time later, he asked her to marry him. She did not want to say yes, once again because of her past life of prostitution, but after hearing of this young man's declaration of love for her, she agreed to marry him.

The two decided they wanted to do this marriage thing right so went to a doctor to see if the girl had incurred any sexually transmitted diseases. After the girl had been checked, the doctor explained to her that to become infected with a sexually transmitted disease a person needed to have sex. The girl was confused and explained to the doctor she had been a prostitute for 15 years and that during that time she had had sex with many men. The doctor reiterated that physically she was a virgin and in order for her to have a sexually transmitted disease, she needed to have sex, which he was convinced she had not.

This story amazes me and I am challenged to take another step forward in understanding the grace of God through Jesus. Isaiah 30:26 says, "The moon will shine like the sun and the sunlight will be seven times brighter, like the light of seven full days, when the Lord binds up the bruises of His people and heals the wounds He inflicted." Whoever this girl is, she is experiencing the grace of God in such a way that we can only stand amazed and say with Habakkuk, "For the earth will be filled with the knowledge of the glory of the Lord, as the waters cover the sea" (2:14).

This young woman needed to be made physically new, but for some of us, we must understand that when we are under the grace of God, life is just as if we had never sinned and if God has said that we are pure and holy, then we are pure and holy. Some of us need to comprehend the truth that we are new because God says so, no matter what others think, even doctors. Surely it was gracious of God to let this young women's desire to be made physically new again help her understand her newness was if it happened in the physical realm. For some of us, we must realize the world in which we live has always been deceiving, that a serpent has been lying to us for a long time and that newness, as defined by God, is enough. We need to understand that since we have been seated with Christ in heaven, we are more pure than we could possibly imagine and the physical realm is only a distorted view of the truth. In this world we may see ourselves as corrupted or impure, but the truth is that we are totally pure and without blemish. We need to understand grace.

Imagine the beginning of creation. Genesis 1:1 says that God created. God did not bend, twist or mold creation; God created creation. In 1:3 God said, "Let there be light," and guess what, there it was. God did not say, "Let light shine," because light did not exist yet. God said, "Let there be light." Then suddenly light, out of nowhere, appeared being light. God spoke light into existence. At one moment some idea, some thing, some being, did not exist and then God spoke and it existed.

This is something God does. He speaks reality into existence and in our cases, because of God's grace, He speaks purity and holiness into our lives, making these a reality. Where once we may not have seen purity, we now see it existing, because God speaks purity. If a door is blue and God says the door is red, then the door is red. Even if the door looks blue, feels blue or even tastes blue, the door is red, because God said it. God speaks newness into our beings. We may not feel new, or perceive newness, but when God speaks, the words God says become reality, because God's words are reality. "Forget the former things; do not dwell on the past. See, I am doing a new thing! Now it springs up; do you not perceive it? I am making a way in the desert and streams in the wasteland" (Is 43:18-19).

According to Titus 1:2, God cannot lie. Because of this, we can agree with Revelation 19:7-9 when it says: "Let us rejoice and be glad and give Him glory! For the wedding of the Lamb has come and His bride has made herself ready. Fine linen, bright and clean, was given her to wear. Then the angel said to me, 'Write: Blessed are those who are invited to the wedding supper of the Lamb!'" And he added, "These are the true words of God."

What if our knowledge of God's glory gained us the wisdom to understand what it means to be the bride of Christ and to be swimming in such a grace we know the Lord is our Mighty One and that nothing can come against the place that God has brought us to be a part, as it says in Isaiah 33:21. Because of Christ's blood, we are healed. We need to understand this and proclaim it over our lives. If we are Christ's bride, then God has brought us to a place of untouchable newness where all our wounds have been healed. "No one living in Zion will say, 'I am ill'; and the sins of those who dwell there will be forgiven" (Is 33:24).

When one begins to see the beauty in the truth that they are truly the bride of Christ, then one begins to understand that Jesus will not settle for anyone being less than completely restored, healed and made totally pure. When our time comes to enter the wedding of the Lamb, we will be ready and God will have made it so that we have made ourselves ready by becoming one with Christ. For many of us, sex is what has made us see ourselves as less than pure and so much lower than holiness and sex (oneness with Christ) is what has and will restore us to our proper place and identity. It is our calling to be the bride of Christ, to be one with Him and then to follow wherever He may lead.

I wonder if God is calling all of us to love Him like a bride. I do not want to push my personal experience off on anyone, but I do wonder if God truly is calling us to love Him that way. Maybe He is and maybe some of us do not like the idea, for various reasons. If someone does not like it, I hope it is not because they fear what might not happen if they become immersed in God's empowering grace. God's grace is big. That is why He sent Jesus and gave His glory to only His Son. Isaiah 42:8 says God only gives His glory to Jesus. That is why Jesus came for us, to be one with us. That is why He desires to be our groom. That is why we must become His bride and become one with Him. Is it time for us to love God like a bride?

I look forward to discussing our feminine side before God with you. But remember, this does not mean that you cannot be that ever-respected warrior you have always wanted to be. God wants you to fight, but maybe He also wants you to be swept off of your feet and taken on a journey where someday you may find yourself walking on water.

19

Feet

I am amazed sometimes at the different methods Christians use to bring performance-based religion upon themselves. Many believers use verses like Ephesians 5:10 which tells us to, "Find out what pleases the Lord." I can see the stress and anxiety created when people attempt to cover all of the boundaries in order to make sure they are doing pleasing things, like striving not to sin, ever, and telling others to do the same. When I hear people say, "I just want to please the Lord," I want to scream at the top of my lungs: "You do please the Lord. You please Him because He made you to please Him. Because of His Son you are the most pleasing to Him you will ever be!"

Remember when Jesus' healed the demon-possessed man? Jesus asked him, "What is your name?" "Legion," he replied, because many demons had gone into him. And they begged him repeatedly not to order them to go into the Abyss. A large herd of pigs was feeding there on the hillside. The demons begged Jesus to let them go into them and he gave them permission. When the demons came out of the man, they went into the pigs and the herd rushed down the steep bank into the lake and was drowned. When those tending the pigs saw what had happened, they ran off and reported this in the town and countryside and the people went out to see what had happened. When they came to Jesus, they found the man from whom the demons had gone out, sitting at Jesus' feet, dressed and in his right mind; and they were afraid. Those who had seen it told the people how the demon-possessed man had been cured. Then all the people of the region of the Gerasenes asked Jesus to leave them, because they were overcome with fear. So He got into the boat and left (Lk 8:30-37).

When everyone came to see what Jesus had done, they found the man sitting at Jesus' feet and so they went and told everyone else the man had been cured. Which part do you suppose was more pleasing to Jesus? Was it that this individual had managed to get his life together, get cleaned up, find a good job and make spiritual friends? No, I think that Jesus was pleased to see a man whom He created to sit at his feet, sitting at His feet. Do you wonder what Jesus told the man in those moments he was sitting at His feet? Was it a new name, or what to tell the other people because they would not understand His grace? I don't know, but I trust this man understood that nothing he could do would make him pleasing to Jesus, but that it was Jesus who had created the man to enjoy Him and when he was sitting at Jesus' feet, he was doing exactly that, enjoying Him.

What might have happened if those who told everyone the man had been cured explained he was now sitting at Jesus' feet? Maybe they would have sought Jesus out as he did to be delivered from their fears. Instead, they asked Jesus to leave because they were afraid. The man who had been healed was told to go home and tell what had been done for him. Jesus knew the people there did not understand. They did not see the power of sitting at the feet of Christ. They were afraid so asked Him to leave, which was evidence of not seeking Jesus. Look at Psalm 34:4; "I sought the Lord and He answered me and delivered me from all my fears."

Consider Mary and Martha in John 12:1-3:

Six days before the Passover, Jesus arrived at Bethany, where Lazarus lived, whom Jesus had raised from the dead. Here a dinner was given in Jesus' honor. Martha served, while Lazarus was among those reclining at the table with him. Then

Mary took about a pint of pure nard, an expensive perfume; she poured it on Jesus' feet and wiped his feet with her hair. And the house was filled with the fragrance of the perfume.

There are two activities going on here – Martha is in the kitchen serving and Mary is sitting at Jesus' feet. Martha had probably been preparing all day knowing the Son of God, who raised Lazarus from the dead, was coming to her house. The food is prepared, the house is clean and Martha is still serving, wanting everything to be perfect for Jesus. I wonder how many of us are like Martha? We want to please the Lord and we seek to, but too many times it seems as though no matter what we do, it is never enough.

Take anorexia, a disease that causes people not to eat food at all costs. Nobody wants to be anorexic; we all desire food. We become hungry and we yearn to be filled. However, some do not eat for fear that if they fill their stomachs, they will not be pleasing to themselves or to the people around. But what we really desire as people is relationship – and more than anything we long to experience each other in ways that show our affection, concern and companionship. We like to love and know that we are being loved. With anorexia, we strive to make ourselves pleasing, but in so doing, become so disgustingly consumed with ourselves and how others might look upon us, we do not take the time to relax and actually experience relationship with the people who desire us most and who love us.

I wonder how many of us are, figuratively, anorexic Christians? Are we like Martha, constantly in the kitchen attempting to finish all our duties and make sure that we're pleasing to Jesus? Do we not stop striving, even when the Son of the Most High God is sitting in our living room? Do we actually think we will do something to earn His praise and make us acceptable? Do we think our relationship to Jesus is contingent upon us?

Think about Mary. Some of us might wonder why she, when the Son of Almighty God is visiting, is not in the kitchen like Martha making sure that everything is perfect. I'm sure with all the work Martha was doing, she could have used Mary's help. But no, Mary is in the living room, sitting at Jesus' feet and enjoying Him. I can almost imagine Martha pulling Mary into the kitchen and saying something like, "Mercy, Mary, Jesus is here and all you can do is stare at Him. I'm sure Jesus gets enough attention already. The last thing He wants is for us to have a messy house meanwhile consuming all of His time and energy. Mary, Mary, Mary. Jesus wants us to work. He needs to see how we have got our lives together and how prepared we are when He comes to visit. Don't you know that faith without works is dead? We need to show Jesus our faith is not dead. Now get in here and help me."

Mary desired to enjoy Jesus, to be with Him and to be herself. Jesus desired this, too. It is amazing how many of us think our relationship with God is weighed by what we do or do not do. I am sure Martha, no matter how much she did, could always find more to be done. If the floor was swept, she could wipe down the cupboards. If the cupboards were clean, Martha could make a new dessert. And if everything was prepared and ready, Martha would probably decide to sweep the floor one last time.

In college I heard that as a young priest Martin Luther used to beat himself physically every time he caught himself sinning. He thought nothing he could do would make him acceptable before God. Many hours spent in the confessional did not relieve the consciousness of his own state before God. Then one day Luther learned he could go to God, through Jesus, by faith and discover what God really thought of him. Imagine the relief Luther felt when he read Romans and realized he no longer had to beat himself in order to please God. Luther who was once like Martha, found he could sit at Jesus' feet having done nothing and be accepted for who he was. This type of relationship quickly transformed the church because of one man's willingness to let God speak without first thinking the kitchen, or anything else, needed to be spotless. I wonder what would happen if we did the same?

Jesus urged the weary to come to Him for rest. He didn't demand that first the weary make sure everything is in right order. I can imagine what my life would be like if I had to make sure my kitchen, figuratively speaking, was in order before I could approach Jesus. I would be constantly working, striving and toiling to do the right thing only to find myself repeatedly covering the dirty tracks I made for fear Jesus would know what really went on as I was preparing myself for Him.

I remember one summer trying hard to make myself right before I left for church camp. This grueling preparation process consisted of striving not to sin as much as I could so I could feel good about worshiping God during the evening services and not be forced, out of my own guilt, to go to the back of the room with some guy that I had no relationship with and unveil all of my faults, frailties and wrongful sexual thoughts. I was 15 and for one reason or another I had been programmed as if I were a robot to think my life was all about what I was doing. If I was sinning, I was bad, but if I was going around presenting the seven easy steps to salvation to everyone in sight, which I never did but always felt guilty about, I was good and being good was the best way to know I was capable of worshiping God, or sitting at His feet. Looking back now it seemed odd I should think I needed to prepare myself to come to Jesus, instead of knowing He had already prepared me completely.

I actually remember singing praise songs near the end of the week one summer, thinking, "I will always know that I am saved because of how I feel right now." I thought that even if some days I did not feel like I was a Christian I could always go back to the memory of me with hands lifted high, feeling happiness surge through my body and know I was indeed going to heaven when I died. Needless to say, that theory lasted about two weeks. Back home, I began to spiral downward once again, feeling nothing I could do would be good enough for God, but I could always look forward to the great salvation feeling to be experienced in eleven and one-half months – if I had prepared.

The Sunday morning altar call always seemed to spark my motivation to come to the feet of Christ. To me the altar itself was not this place, rather it had become a kind of mediator so once I had been down on my knees I would feel good enough to approach the feet of Jesus. It did not necessarily matter how I felt that morning. Some days I would find it hard to approach the altar out of fear what others might think. I could imagine the older women reaching into their purses, searching for stones, knowing what I had been thinking throughout the week. I wondered what the holier men thought of me as I walked my way down the aisle and dropped to my knees. Did these people see me as a sinner, a saint or someone who was just trying hard but could not, for the life of me, get it together? Then I prayed.

Usually my prayers went something like, "Jesus, please forgive me for sinning again. I really don't want to but then I feel like I want to half of the time. I know that I do not deserve to be here, but I don't want to struggle with this sin anymore. Please restore my relationship with You." I would then stay on my knees until my ankles started to hurt. When I could not take any more pain, I would walk back to my seat, wondering what all the people staring at me were thinking. At this point in my life I began to wonder if my desire to be right before God was becoming less about what Jesus had done for me and more about what I was doing out of fear of what God or other people might think.

Things didn't change when I graduated from high school and went off to college. I attended two different Christian colleges and I remember when the altar calls started to really get to me. The first school I attended spent a lot of time talking about becoming sanctified, not as if it were a process, but as if sanctification occurred at a moment in time when a person was prayed through enough and finally reached a higher spiritual level that would help them excel in one's faith faster and more effectively than before. I would go to the altar and pray, telling God I wanted all of Him and that I was willing to do whatever He wanted in order to get all of Him and be constantly at His feet. I usually waited until I started to feel good and then get up and go back to my seat hoping this time was different than the others and that somehow I had reached this state of spiritual efficacy, or power.

Once after a revival service at this school an acquaintance told me that a couple of years before he had gotten sanctified but it wasn't until a couple of months prior that he realized he really wasn't, so he had gone down to the altar again and received his sanctification. He now felt that it was not until a couple of weeks before this revival service that he again went to the altar and got sanctified, this time for real.

As I listened to him describe this cycle he had found himself in, I wondered how much of his motivation to become "sanctified" was coming from a belief he needed to overcome sin in order to find himself holy, set apart for God, or worthy to worship among the fellowship of believers. What would it mean to him to know what Jesus had done for him on the cross? I wanted to tell him that all his strivings were for naught – because of the resurrection.

Somehow I didn't know how to convey this Gospel to one who thought his relationship with God depended on going to the altar repeatedly, hoping each trip would be the final one. I wanted to scream "It is finished," to let him know Christ had accomplished all. However, before the words could leave my tongue, I realized my life was no different from the strivings of my friend. I was searching for a holiness I defined as sinless perfection and each time I failed I would strive harder to overcome my weaknesses so I might get back to the feet of Christ. All the while, I did not comprehend that because of God's grace, when I was weak I was truly strong. This went on for almost two years. Constantly I wondered why, even after the cross, Christians still lived performance-based lives and then I would realize I was doing the same.

At the end of these two years of college, I had a chance to be a sponsor for a high school church camp with a youth group where I volunteered. I sat in the camp meeting hall on "Holy Spirit Night" as the evening speaker told students how much they needed more of the Holy Spirit in their lives. I watched in shock as students came down to the altar wanting more of God. I wanted to scream that Christ had made us all that we need to be when He rose from the dead and gave us His Spirit as a deposit guaranteeing our future with Him, but part of me wanted to go down to the altar with the youth, just in case. I ended up getting out of my chair and walking around to the boys I was sponsoring. As students fell to the ground in front of us I asked a couple of them what they thought of what was happening. They said they did not know so I asked if they felt unspiritual since they were not down front with the others. They said yes; I was feeling the same way.

That night in our room we talked about one of the Greek words for life, *zoe,* used in Romans 8:11 which says, "And if the Spirit of Him who raised Jesus from the dead is living in you, He who raised Christ from the dead will also give life to your mortal bodies through His Spirit, who lives in you." I explained to the boys that when we receive Christ's Spirit as our deposit for eternal life, we also receive this *zoe* life, which is exactly what the speaker for that night was referring to when he talked about receiving a bigger portion of the Holy Spirit, as if He were some kind of three course dinner, instead of a being with a personality.

It dawned on me then how badly I wanted to pull myself out of this performance-based not-so-Christian mentality. I wasn't sure what it was I needed to discover in my relationship with God, but I did know I did not want it to be contingent upon what I did, or how many times I found myself praying at the altar. If it was true that Christ was in me, than maybe I was always before Him sitting at His feet.

Remembering a Forgotten Grace

20

Constant

I remember sitting in a church one Sunday morning during high school, listening to the pastor preach about true love waiting. I had heard many people say things that led me to believe that if a person waited to have sex until they were married then that person would have more to offer their spouse when they finally married. I wanted to give my future spouse all of me, so I waited as hard as I could, when I felt motivated to, but there was always a haunting question in my mind.

I had read Matthew 5:28 where Jesus explained that even by looking at another lustfully, one had committed adultery in their heart. I knew I had done that. I reasoned, because of my failings, I had two directions I could take with my beliefs. I could choose to compare myself with all of those I knew who had chosen not to wait until marriage to have sex – and feel superior because I had not gone as far as they in terms of physical acts.

There was a slight problem with this pattern of thinking because if I did truly choose to think of myself and others in the context of what we had and had not done with our bodies, making our future relationships with others dependent upon these choices, then I would be limiting the Gospel to stretch as far as the east is from the west only in the spiritual realm, leaving the physical and emotional side of life to be experienced in a land of regret. I knew Romans 8:28 said, "And we know that in all things God works for the good of those who love Him, who have been called according to His purpose," yet the temptation for me was to turn Christ's Gospel into a moral checklist which allowed me to feel superior to others based on choices of the past.

It was like saying God's grace was not encompassing enough to include those who had made bad choices, which included me. And this came down to whether or not I could give all of me to God, because I knew if I could do that, then He would take me, all of me, no matter how soiled, dirty or disgusting I thought I had become. This was option two. I chose option two.

The struggle with giving all of me to God came with the teaching that if I was defiled sexually then I could not give all of me to my future spouse. I wondered why so many in the church taught that even though we, by God's grace, are able to give all of ourselves to God, sin and all, we are still not good enough for marital relationships with each other if we had chosen not to wait. Then it struck me that maybe we do not want the bad in relationships. In fact, maybe all we really want from others is for them to make us happy and they can do that best if they have done nothing to hurt us, including before they have known us.

I started to think about God. If all of this is true and if what we are searching for is happiness and people that will never hurt us, then why did God allow Adam and Eve to sin? If God's desire was the same as ours, why didn't he create people to not sin so they could come to Him untainted, without blemish and make God happy, leaving no room for feelings of rejection?

People have argued about this for a long time. Some believe that God allowed Adam and Eve to sin so they could have free will and then when they finally decided to love Him, it would be with their whole hearts, by their choice. Others say God had a sovereign hand on the whole process and it was all part of a plan to send Jesus to the earth and glorify Him through humankind.

Personally, I didn't care if it was choice A, B, or none of the above, I just wanted to know why it was so difficult for us to accept others, maybe even our future spouses, if they had made poor choices in the past. Why were we telling our children to wait so they could later give all of themselves to someone else who had waited, thus sending the message to others that if one had not waited then they had nothing to offer? Why was God accepting all of us, including the bad, but we could only accept from one another that which made us happy? Maybe the problem wasn't in our not being able to receive each other in the same way God received us, but rather in not understanding what it meant for a person to become the bride of Christ. Maybe we were only showing grace to the extent we believed it was being given to us.

Contemplating these concepts, I began to understand why so many of us could not talk about our pasts and when we did speak of poor choices we had made we talked as if they were never a big deal. We were hoping if we could either not talk about our pasts or only talk about them as being insignificant, then maybe our history would not matter to the people we wanted to love us. What we truly desired was to be loved for who we were, not for what we had or had not done – so we wanted the past not to matter. However, the problem was that it did matter to us even though we wanted our sins not to matter to others and us in the same way they did not matter to God because of Jesus.

What would our Christian experience be if we truly began to embrace the truth of Isaiah 43:18-19, "Forget the former things; do not dwell on the past. See, I am doing a new thing! Now it springs up; do you not perceive it? I am making a way in the desert and streams in the wasteland." Could one find it possible to forget the former things and not dwell on their past? Could one really embrace the new things God was doing in one's life as opposed to all of the bad things they had done?

So I began to question what life really was like for someone who had embraced the truth of what had actually occurred when they had become Jesus' bride. I wanted that life because it was one that had me swimming in a pool of grace that was deeper than I had ever known. I wanted to be swept off of my feet by this grace. I could see this newness springing up and I wanted to perceive it and know what it meant to be the bride of Christ, not just in my mind, but also in my very being. I wanted to know what it meant to be new and have this newness be unchanging, or constant.

Think about God. Scriptures tell us God is unchanging. So since the beginning of creation when He spoke the earth into existence, when water was separated from land and the sun was made to shine, all the way until today, God has not changed. He is constant. I used to have friends in elementary school that would be my best friend until I said something wrong or we began liking the same girl. I used to wonder why such little things would cause people to go from being friends to not being friends, back and forth until everyone was hurting or mad. The same scenario happened in high school to the couples who would date, break up, date someone else and break up again. Finally I realized the problem was not that complicated. We were all constantly changing. One year a girlfriend broke up with me so she could date another guy. She told me things were not working out between us but then I noticed they were working out with someone else two days later. Her feelings changed and although at first I did not feel the same way as she did, my feelings soon adapted to my circumstances and I was comfortable with being single for a while.

For me it worked the same with girls as with God. Some days I could go to church and worship God because I felt like I loved Him. Usually, during those times I was happy because He had provided for me, my human relationships were in good standing, or I just felt holy enough to be with a community in worship. Other days I was confused because I did not have a clue what was going on in my life. I could have been hurting, wondering why God had taken me out of a relationship, or just mad because I disagreed with the way things were going. I am a changing individual and my attitude toward God changes daily. If someone were to ask me to give them one word to describe God in my life one day and another word on another day, the words would not be the same because from day to day, I am not the same. I change. God doesn't change.

Imagine if God did change. I have a hard time picturing God deciding one day not to love me anymore because I have not been as good as I should have been. I don't think I would understand what was going on because God would be contradicting His own words which say He will never leave me nor forsake me. Ultimately God can make promises to us like that one because He is confident in the truth that He is unchanging. Malachi 3:6 says, "I the LORD do not change. So you, O descendant of Jacob, are not destroyed." Basically, if God changed, we would be destroyed because when God does not love us, we cannot exist. The absence of His love is a place of destruction. God does not change and because of that we are not destroyed. "Because of the Lord's great love we are not consumed, for His compassions never fail. They are new every morning; great is your faithfulness" (Lam 3:22-23).

God is also continually making things new. In Isaiah 42:9 God says, "See, the former things have taken place and new things I declare; before they spring into being I announce them to you." We cannot change the past, but we can be reminded that God is bringing new things into our lives continually and because of His grace, we are constantly being made new. The past is finished and new things are being declared. Our challenge is coming from Isaiah 43:18-19. We must perceive the newness God is bringing into our lives and forget the former things. Newness is springing up and streams are beginning to form in what was once the driest desert of our lives.

God is continually making things new and His desire is to inject Himself into our very beings so we can perceive what is becoming of all that we really are. God loves us like we are His own bride. But is it possible for us to love God under this blanket of grace and newness? Can we truly forget the former things? Will God save us from our pain if we ask Him to make us new? I believe the answer is yes and that God is calling us to assume our identity in Him. We are called to be Christ's bride and to love Him as a bride in the love that brings grace and newness and love.

I wish I could say that I knew exactly what to do in order to pursue Christ as His bride, but I did not. I wish I could say that there was someone in my life who directed me to the exact place I needed to be every moment, but there was not. All I knew was that God was calling me to love Him like a bride and I knew I wanted to cross the threshold between all of my strivings to be acceptable before God, poetically speaking about strange romantic experiences with our Creator, to actually being swept off of my feet and brought into a relationship where two beings are so immersed into one moment with each other they can be mistaken as one. I wanted that with God but I was not sure how to get it or if I already had it and just had not recognized its existence. I knew definitely I wanted that kind of relationship. I wanted to be Christ's bride. That is when I started to think about sex.

21

Heart

"Take me away with you–let us hurry! Let the king bring me into his chambers" (Song 1:4). I've heard that the inner chamber of a king, during medieval times and before was extremely exclusive. Few were allowed to enter into a king's bedroom and if someone was, it had better have been because of an invitation, or at least an understanding that he would pay later with his life.

I cannot begin to imagine the feelings of a woman who, possibly in love with a king, was swept into his inner chamber. Of course, there were probably few women throughout history who actually wanted to approach a king in his bedroom. But if a woman was in love and married, this would be a wondrous experience. The inner chamber was an intimate place.

This is what amazes me about the book of Esther. Here she is, the bride of the king yet she is not allowed to see her own husband without an invitation. However, because of God's leading, Esther risks her life and saves her people. She makes it to the king's inner chamber. We know Esther had previously been taken there, but when the crucial moment arose, it is almost as if she knows where she belongs. I can picture her standing before her husband with the strength similar to Moses' saying, "Husband, let my people go!" I'm sure that it did not happen quite like that.

Either way, the king's inner chamber was an intimate place and yes, that is where people had sex.

As I thought about this concept of the inner chamber, I began to wonder if it was possible to have sex with another person and yet not allow them into one's personal inner chamber. Was there really a way to give oneself away physically without actually giving oneself away? I thought of all the people who had allowed themselves to become physically intimate with someone else, in an attempt to become in love or at least believe they were. Was it possible to be "one" with more than one person? The thought had me perplexed. I knew in Old Testament times people had sex to confirm a marriage and we still do that today. Yet did King Solomon, the wisest man ever to live, become "one" with all of his various wives and concubines? Had he truly given himself away to all of them? I discovered quickly that the answer was no. King Solomon was "one" with no one. He had a divided heart as is evident by this passage:

> [Solomon] had 700 wives of royal birth and 300 concubines and his wives led him astray. As Solomon grew old, his wives turned his heart after other gods and his heart was not fully devoted to the Lord his God, as the heart of David his father had been (1 Ki 11:3-4).

Think of Solomon's wives sitting around him with their many books on philosophy, logic and world religions, debating Solomon day and night until finally, one day, he decided some of their gods were just as good as his and he should accommodate these idols. I do not think this happened. However, Solomon, in all his wisdom, for some reason did not allow himself to be romanced by the true Creator of the universe. He had a divided heart and was therefore one with no one, not even God. Solomon had sex with many women, but he never allowed himself to become intimate with his true Groom. Unlike his father David, Solomon did not know what it meant to be the bride of Christ.

The difference between Solomon and David was that Solomon's heart was divided whereas David's heart was devoted. David had allowed the Creator of the universe to sweep him off of his feet. Although David made plenty of mistakes in his lifetime, he had an open, honest and intimate relationship with his Father and because of that, an undivided heart. David's prayer was simple after he committed adultery with Bathsheba. He wanted his heart to be one with God's and to have intimacy restored. Unlike Solomon, even after he had given himself physically to another, David knew that without an intimate connection with his Father he would find himself divided and looking in all of the wrong places to quench his passionate hunger. Here is part of David's prayer: "Create in me a pure heart, O God, and renew a steadfast spirit within me" (Ps. 51:10).

Not only did David want his heart to be solely God's, but he also desired to have a steadfast spirit so in times of temptation and trouble he could know and act according to Whom his heart belonged. David desired God's heart; Solomon was seeking to have his heart filled up without the struggle. The difference is the same as drinking water from a clean well versus a toilet that has not been flushed in days. One has to dig a well in order to get fresh water, but to create a toilet all one has to do is urinate.

I wonder how many of us like Solomon have found ourselves drinking out of the toilet, trying to quench our spiritual thirst for God? I've heard people say it is hard to know how to turn to God for fulfillment because it is not like He is standing around the next corner, waiting to give us a hug. I've heard girls say they cannot touch God, but they can touch their boyfriends and I have even had similar thoughts. Then I asked myself, is my heart divided? Out of how many more toilets do I need to drink before I truly figure out I need to allow God to pursue me as His bride? When I am finally ready to love God like a bride, how do I go about doing it? Then the truth hit me. The only reason we love God is undoubtedly because He first loved us.

Our desire to be loved in return for our giving of love is a desire that flows to us directly from the heart of God. Many times we do not do the greatest job in actually loving others who loved us first. Nevertheless, we do hope, with the deepest part of our souls, that when we put our hearts on the line and speak words which bring all that we know about acceptance and relationship to a climax offering them to another, we will hear the same words repeated to us. We have this hope that instead of experiencing the utmost rejection, we might possibly find someone willing to love us back. We desire that moment when two people know they are in the same place, not only physically, but spiritually and emotionally as well.

We long for these moments of intimate connection because they sweep us off of our feet. They leave us free falling. The problem comes when we find ourselves being caught up in a rush of emotion hoping the person next to us understands our experience and instead of communicating it, we pretend the person is in synchrony with our experience. We find ourselves not in a true unconditional relationship, but rather one where two people do whatever it takes to stay looking good, keep feelings alive and make sure their significant-other is in constant appreciation of what they are doing to selfishly find fulfillment, at the risk of damaging the other's heart. This is the difference between a divided and a devoted heart.

The first time I told a girl that I loved her it was not the same as when I had told God that I loved Him. As a matter of fact, the love that I was speaking into my girlfriend, at the time, was much stronger, more passionate and definitely more devoted than the words coming out of my mouth when I spoke to God. I wanted this girl to know I loved her. More than anything I wanted her to know that. I wanted this girl to understand that, in my mind, I would have gone to the deepest part of the ocean if it would have helped to convey my love for her. I wanted more than anything for her to receive my love and find joy in the truth that she was captivatingly loveable to me.

I knew how I wanted to be loved. I wanted a girl who was willing to go wherever I went and follow me like a bride follows her groom into the inner chamber. I wanted a girl who, after seeing me for all that I was, loved me and wanted nothing more than to spend time allowing me to cherish, bless and treat her like she deserved to be treated. In that moment I realized my desires were not different from those that come from the heart of God. God knew how He wanted to be loved. He wanted me to be willing to go wherever He would lead me and follow Him everywhere He went, just like a bride follows her groom. God wanted me to see Him for all that He was, in all of His glory, splendor, power, might, majesty, gentleness and love and allow Him to show me what experiencing all of His qualities was like. God wanted me to love Him in the exact ways I was desiring to be loved.

This revelation was powerful to me and I wondered why I had missed such a concept for so many years. God wanted me to love Him like I wanted to be loved by a girl. I finally began to understand. God had created me to feel because He felt. He created me to love because He loved. God created me to cherish someone someday because He cherished me today. I had been created to receive the love of God because He wanted me to experience all that He had to offer. After receiving this great gift, more romantic than all desires and passions, He wanted me to give it all back to Him as freely as His love had been received. At that moment I thought maybe I was going to get that romantic happy ending my heart had been desiring for so long.

I remembered stories from my youth about damsels in distress. Usually the damsel was a gorgeous beauty trapped in a castle or under some kind of spell and she was waiting to be rescued by her knight in shining armor – or perhaps someone who looked more like Robin Hood. No matter what he always came. The princess was always rescued and everyone always lived happily ever after.

Now I realize why people in the stories always live happily ever after – because whoever was telling these stories never spoke of what happened after the moment when the mighty knight came to rescue the princess. Usually there was a battle, a conquering of evil, a party, a kiss and then the story ended with those famous three words, "happily ever after." These stories always had happy endings because they were always stuck in the same moment.

No one ever talked about what happened when Snow White went home with her prince and lived the rest of her life compulsively studying her food carefully before eating, especially fruit. No one ever mentioned that although she moved away from her evil stepmother and sisters, Cinderella had to speak with a counselor for years to learn how to cope with feelings of rejection and abandonment. [Just kidding.] Seriously, these stories always ended just before reality set in and I wondered if because of that, we were constantly searching for an endless moment of romantic ecstasy. If this were truly what we were looking for then why were we not trying to find it in our consistently new and never-changing God?

What bothers me about Christians is how we tend to speak of God as if He were some type of super-cool parent who, although full of grace and truth, does nothing more than hand out blessings when we ask for stuff. We think if we conform to a list of ideas, we have a relationship with Jesus and then we tell others that, if they think like us, they can also be in relationship with God.

What if our relationship with God were more of a romance and less of a checklist? What if what God really wanted from us, instead of striving to do or not do different acts, was for us to receive His love, enjoy it and by doing that let Him know we truly love Him back? What if our relationship with God was less like a chore and more like a dance? What if we could wake up in the morning and dance with God all day? What if asking us to dance is what God has been doing all this time, but instead of romantically allowing Him to carry us around the room with strong, yet graceful, movements of love and passion, we have been wasting our time striving to find the right clothes for fear that, even though we are Christ's bride, captivatingly radiant to Him, we are not good enough to waltz with our Groom? What if, even though all of this is going on, He is still asking us to dance? What if God will continue waiting until we finally say yes to just one dance? What if just one dance is all that Jesus needs to romance our hearts and sweep us off of our feet? What if that dance could be the never-ending, ever joyous, helplessly romantic moment that we have been trying to find in everything and everyone else? What if all that we need to do, in order to find out if what God is truly offering us is all that we hope it to be, is say yes—and dance? I hope we dance.

I hope we dance because I believe that romance is what our relationship with Jesus Christ, the Son of the Most High God, is all about. I hope we dance so we can know what the experience is like. I hope we choose to dance with our Father because in the midst of all the muck, trash and filth of life, God has broken through our rusty cell doors and asked us to allow Him to spin us hypnotically around His inner chamber. Romance with God is what I believe we were created for and, although we have found ourselves looking in every other corner of every other room, He has persistently pursued us with an unchangingly new and passionate desire for just one dance, just one song. Hear the words of a devoted heart. In Psalm 30:11 David says, "You turned my wailing into dancing; You removed my sackcloth and clothed me with joy."

22

Dreams

Waking up to the cool breeze of free air pouring through her window in the locked tower was nothing new for Isabel. She had been trapped in the castle for as long as she could remember and freedom, although experienced while running through open fields of green grass during dreams, was a reality too distant to touch her present state. Once awake Isabel would fix her hair, straighten her dress and then spend the rest of the day staring out the tower window into the nearby forest wondering what life might be like were she somehow to transcend her limited existence.

The forest was amazing, as far as Isabel could tell. The trees seemed to be as tall as the castle. The grass was the greenest green she had ever seen. Every morning the sun came up over the tree line, making each tree sing with the beauty of a freedom Isabel had yet to experience. How she longed to run and play in the green grass, swim in the waterfalls and dry off in the warmth of the rising sun. She told herself if she ever did make her way to the tree line of the massive forest, she would enter it and never return. With all that was in her, Isabel desired to be free of the castle walls around her and run with the joy of the unending freedom which she glimpsed whenever she stared out her open window.

The castle which entombed Isabel was also gigantic, although it did not possess the freedom of the forest. Isabel never left the upstairs tower. In fact, she could not leave. Isabel wondered if it was a giant dragon that had her locked in her tower and if someday a knight in shining armor would come, slay the dragon and sweep her off of her feet – if there even was a dragon in the first place. Isabel hated the castle.

Isabel did not know why she had been trapped in the castle for as long as she could remember. In fact, she could not recall even a brief moment of her life before she had been unconsciously sentenced to spend the rest of her days in loneliness and self-saturation. All she did know was that every day she woke up, fixed her hair, fixed her dress and waited, not knowing exactly why she waited, but wait she did. It was as if something in the forest, a freedom beyond her own experience, beckoned her to come outside each day she stared out of her lofty window. Isabel would wait intently and stare with anxious excitement for the day when she could finally go farther than the glimpses of the far-away tree line. She longed to become part of the freedom that would surround her being if she ever found herself outside of her castle walls and immersed into the new, dangerous and freeing woods.

Many days Isabel tried to escape through the locked door in her room. There was a key hole through which she could see into the inner parts of the castle and she thought that if somehow she could get through the door and inside the castle then she could possibly find her way outside. She attempted to pick the lock but found it was too heavy and had been welded shut. Isabel tried to pry the wooden boards away from the door, but found they were too thick and heavy for one person to move, much less pry loose from the huge door. Isabel despised that door.

Usually Isabel, when not staring out of her window, would sit on the floor by the locked door and scream that whoever was keeping her in the room needed to let her go because she had done nothing wrong. Some days she would get tired of defending her own standing before whomever it was who had trapped her into her cell and blame that person with loud complaints of unjust punishment and torture. Sometimes Isabel even pretended she was not locked inside of a tiny room and would prance about in the way she thought a horse running free in the undiscovered woods would, but usually she did not prance long due to the limited space in the room. Running in circles made Isabel dizzy. Isabel hated the castle.

One time Isabel attempted to climb down the side of her tower wall, but her bed sheets were not long enough and she barely made it ten feet below her window. She contemplated jumping, but the only times before when she had jumped were in her dreams and Isabel knew her dreams were not real. If she were to jump in real life she might possibly die and if she died, she did not know where she would find herself. She did not want to die, but at the same time, she did not want to live if she had to remain in the tower for the rest of her days.

In the castle, Isabel's days were monotonous. She would sleep all night, wake in the morning, fix her hair and her dress and wait, even though she did not know why she waited. She did find glimpses of freedom when she stared out her window, but that was not the most enjoyable part of her existence. Isabel loved to dream. Every evening after watching the light of the forest fade into a pitch black (for the sun set on the back side of the castle) Isabel would run to her bed, cover herself if the night promised to be cold, place her head on her pillows and fall asleep as quickly as possible. Some nights Isabel was so eager to get to sleep that it evaded her for hours, but when sleep came she was immediately swept away from the immovable castle walls and into the joyous freedom of the massive forest where she would run and play as long as she could, usually until she was so tired her muscles ached and forced her to stop whatever she was doing and lay in the greenest green grass slowly fading, until she was asleep in her

Remembering a Forgotten Grace

dream.

Although Isabel loved to sleep which took her into the dream world of the forest in the first place, she did not like the rude awakening she received every time she dozed off while in the forest, for she would always awake in her tiny, closed-in castle room which she could not leave. Isabel hated her castle, but she loved her dreams.

One morning, after a long night of romping and playing in the forest, Isabel awoke to find grass stains on her dress and dandelions in her hair. The night before she had dreamed of wandering into the forest and finding the most beautiful creatures. She had taken flowers and placed them in her hair, climbed trees and swam in waterfalls. Isabel had even rolled down a hill of tall green grass that was softer than any pillow on which she had ever laid her head. Isabel looked at her dress in amazement and held the flowers as if they were precious jewels from another world. Never had something like this happened before. It was as if her dream had come true, or at least parts of it were invading her present reality, changing all she knew about herself, life and freedom.

Soon after Isabel's first dream had come true, she began to experience more and more mysterious happenings. One morning she awoke to find a pony nibbling at her ear. Another morning she was shocked to find a fresh garden of beautiful daisies growing atop her pillow. Isabel was astounded. Her dreams were becoming real and entering into her seemingly simple existence. After a while, Isabel began to wonder which existence she was living was actually real? She thought the castle room was all she had known in the past and she had definitely spent time trapped behind those walls, but the dream forest was the only place where Isabel found herself really alive. The forest was abundant with life; the castle was not. Isabel wanted, more than anything else, to believe her dream world was real and that her castle was a dream, but on the surface she knew otherwise. She had been convinced her entire life that dreams were not real and that experience was nothing more than that which was around you when you were the most aware.

She began to contemplate what it was that made her most aware and alive. She decided she knew she was alive in the castle because of the pain she felt and the hope she possessed. She concluded she definitely had feelings when she was in the castle and even though they were similar to a roller coaster, going back and forth from fulfilled dreams to disappointed hopes, Isabel knew she could not deny these feelings. When she was in the forest, her life was suddenly no longer about how she felt. She would run and play, but the joy that came from knowing she was free was much more than any feeling Isabel had ever experienced. That joy was increasing more than all of the feelings upon which she had based her life while living in the castle. In the forest, Isabel had found a place of freedom which existed beyond her emotional fickleness and there she was fully aware and fully alive. Isabel loved her forest.

The forest was far more beautiful than anything Isabel had ever imagined. The trees were tall and powerful. The grass was soft beneath her toes and all of the animals were friendly. Isabel loved her forest. She would run through the grass, feeling the wind against her face and when it rained she would dance. Isabel loved the rain, but she also loved the sunshine. When the sun came out every morning Isabel would swim in the waterfalls and then nap on the rocks while she dried her clothes.

At first when Isabel napped she would dream of a far off and distant land where she was not free. Sometimes these dreams would last for days. In this land Isabel was trapped in a room where she could not run in the forest. In fact, she could not even leave the room. Isabel would wake up in sadness, but then look at the sun and joy would pierce her heart. It was as if she desired to run and play instead of sleep because of these nightmares. Isabel decided, because of all of the bad dreams, she would always stay awake as long as possible in order to enjoy her freedom in the woods, without having to wrestle with the horrible imaginations of her mind. Isabel's soul had been awakened and although she did find herself tired at times, deep down in her heart she decided being awake was far better than remaining in a constant torturing slumber.

In the forest Isabel was finally living her dream. She transcended her experience of continual loneliness, hopelessness and self-saturation and had begun living in a place that was far more than words could express. She was now in a place where defending herself against all of her imagined accusations was unnecessary and pretending she was not trapped in a castle was a game she no longer needed. She was in the forest and she was free. In the past, Isabel had seen glimpses of this freedom when she looked out of her open tower window and although she had not yet experienced this joy she did not lose hope and she never stopped dreaming. Isabel's dreams became her reality and she was finally swept off her feet, out of her castle and into her ever new, ever joyous, ever free and always unchanging reality.

However, Isabel did not live happily ever after. Many times she stubbed her toes on rocks while running through the greenest green grass. Sometimes the sun was not as hot as she desired, especially in winter, so she could not dry off quickly and she faced the difficulty of remaining wet all day. Some days Isabel was sick because of the plants she ate and other days she spent many hours caring for sick animals, with no time to play. Isabel did not live happily ever after, but since she was in the forest, Isabel learned not to rely on her emotions. She was free and the joy of this freedom was much greater than a feeling, although it was much different. Isabel had been swept off of her feet and set back down in a place where the joyous freedom of unchanging newness was all that mattered all the time. She had been placed in a forest and the funny part was that there was no glorious knight in shining armor she could touch, kiss, or ask to dance. It was almost as if her Savior was everywhere. He had slowly crept into her mind and taken her from the cave of her castle walls and into the forest where her heart had always dwelled. Isabel could not see Him but she knew He was there, everywhere and He was the one keeping her free.

Every second, for Isabel, became a dance with her Savior, the one who had awakened her soul. When she ran barefoot in the grass she danced with Him. When she bathed in the waterfalls she danced with Him. When she played with the animals and climbed the colossal trees she danced with Him. Even when she dried off in the sun, she danced with Her savior. This was a new experience for Isabel. She was in a new place she had never been and she was in that new place every day. Isabel could not understand this unchanging newness; she could only accept it. All she knew was that she was new, that she was in this forest and that she was dancing with her Savior. From that moment on, when Isabel was with her Savior, nothing else mattered.

Part Four

Joy in Mourning

23

Jesus

I used to think that I remembered the day I was born. My sister Kelly and I argued about this when we were younger. When I remembered a curly-haired doctor with glasses, Kelly said that was because our mom told me that. I would say that the room was half green and half white, with the green half being tiles that went down to the floor. Kelly would say that was how all delivery rooms looked. I would say that I remembered bright lights. Kelly would roll her eyes. I honestly do not think I really ever had a convincing argument. Maybe I just liked to argue.

I have three sisters total, but I like to think that I have four: Lisa, Christie, Kelly and Renee. I say that Renee is my sister because I really cannot look a her any other way. She is my oldest two sisters' sister and when I first met her she taught me, through my observations of her and Kelly, how to use nun-chucks. What are sisters for, right? Now I know how to defend myself against a black ninja death warrior if I can somehow grab his nun-chucks before I get hit with a deadly Chinese star.

Lisa is my oldest and wisest sister. At least that's what I say. She, her husband Doug and their son Michael lived in New York until recently when they moved to be closer to my parents in South Dakota. I see Lisa as wise because, no matter what I tell her about what is going on in my life, she usually responds with the exact words I need to hear. Whenever I have had girl problems, she was always the one who helped me the most. I have never admitted that before, but I am coming out with it now. I do not think anyone will mind – that much. She went away to Germany with the Air Force when I was little, so I really do not remember much about our early relationship.

Christie, my middle sister, was probably the funniest. At least I thought she was because we had almost the exact same sense of humor. I can imagine how hard it was for her having me around, especially with the age difference, but ultimately I think she did a good job, with the cards she was dealt. I never really liked it when Christie would baby-sit me because I always got in trouble. Once, I remember getting in trouble right after my parents had left and then having to wait through the rest of the evening knowing I was going to get spanked when they got home. I felt like I was part of a cheesy movie that everyone knew how it was going to end. Everyone would sit watching this movie in suspense as I sat in the back frustrated. "Come on guys, everyone knows what's going to happen. Rod gets spanked." I liked Christie more as a sister and less as a baby-sitter, although contrary to my opinion at the time, I did need a baby-sitter. Four-year-olds know everything right? It truly was nice having two older sisters with a lot of life experience to help me when I wound up in places I wished I would never have found. Later in life, Christie helped me most when I did not have a clue what I was going to do with my life. I love my sisters.

Kelly was definitely my closest sister. In all reality, we grew up together, moved to Kansas with our parents after our other sisters had been long gone, cried together and protected each other from boys and girls who had deceptive interests. To me our relationship was pretty funny because, if people did not know we were brother and sister in college, they would have thought that we were dating. And might I add they would have thought I had quite the catch. But we weren't dating and after four or five guys told Kelly God had told them they were supposed to be together, she got engaged and married a guy who did not say such words. The wedding was hard for me, but I think it is cool to see two people come together who are absolutely perfect for each other.

My mom used to tell me a story about the day when she first came home with me from the hospital. She had been gone for a while and Kelly was quite jealous. She stood on the front porch of our trailer with her Raggedy Ann doll, hands on her hips, with an angry face which said she wanted everyone to know how mad she was. In my opinion, my sister and I had a good first encounter, although I was a baby and couldn't tell myself from the car in which I rode home. I told Kelly I remembered that day. She still did not believe me.

I never had any brothers growing up, but a cousin of mine did live with us for awhile until he got tired and moved. I remember he got kicked out of school for something and then my parents sent him to a treatment center. When he got out he decided he did not want to live with us anymore – which I think was a bad choice. Ultimately, my parents were trying to help him work through his issues and he decided to run from his issues, instead. I haven't talked to him in a long time. I do trust God, however, to bring him back around.

My parents, Craig and Diane, met in a drug- and alcohol-reha-bilitation center, then they got married. My mom told me how my dad swept her off of her feet by bringing her vanilla ice cream, which she loved, as they were both sitting in the commons area of the facility. She responded to this kind and romantic gesture by asking my dad if he was finished having kids. Two years after my parents got married, little Rod was born. I was the youngest in my family. I love my parents.

Before I was born and moved in, my parents lived in a trailer house with my sisters. There was a pastor at the local community church who constantly visited our home to talk to my parents about whatever it was that they wanted to discuss. Usually, my dad wanted to debate about the Bible and so they would converse back and forth until it was time for this pastor to leave. I suspect this pastor wondered why he drove his car out to the middle of nowhere in order to argue with two long-haired recovering hippies who wanted to tell him that the way he read the Bible was not the way that it should be read. What I liked about hearing my parents tell this story was that no matter what, this pastor never failed to darken the doorstep of this seemingly motley crew, week after week.

Once when this pastor showed up for another onslaught of questions and debate, the house was in turmoil. My dad had been in an argument with one of my sisters and did not know what to do. I can't recall what the argument was about, but I do know everyone in the house was flipping out. My dad explained the situation to the pastor but I do not know if anyone ever reached a decision on how to handle the matter, yet by the time this pastor left, he had spoken some of the most powerful words our family, even to this day, had ever heard. I say this because of the implications and drastic change which ensued.

The pastor looked my dad straight in the eyes and said, "You know, you could spit in Jesus' face right now and He would still love you." Then he left. Immediately my parents got down on their knees and gave all they knew how to give to God, because of all they knew Jesus had done, was doing and would do in them and their family for the rest of their lives. I was not born until after my parents had known this God for a year and I am thankful they met Him when they did.

I have always wondered what my testimony would sound like if I were asked to speak in front of the entire world. I have heard people in the past tell stories of how God delivered them from prostitution, drugs, alcohol, gang violence or a combination of these, which made me wonder why people would even care to hear about my life and the change that may have seemed so insignificant, when I was four years old. I remember it vividly.

As my mother and I arrived home one day, as we pulled into the driveway I felt the Holy Spirit in my being. This was the first time I had experienced the Holy Spirit, but I recognized the sensation, if it even was a sensation. In that moment, although I could not put the experience into as elegant words as I can today, I knew I was not my own and just like the Bible says, I was definitely bought with the price of God's Son, Jesus. I knew if I let God take whatever it was He wanted, then He would never leave me and in that moment, I did not want Him to leave. My parents had talked to me before about sin, heaven, hell and Jesus, so I knew some of the words to say. I turned to my mom and asked her if I could ask Jesus into my heart.

As I recall, my mother got pretty excited, explained to me once again that I was a sinner and that Jesus could forgive my sins, making it clear it was my sins which He wanted to take away from me and that I would get to be with God in heaven someday. I prayed with my mom and then seven angels came down from above bearing gifts of great value, which my family sold and lived happily ever after off of the money that we made.

Just kidding. I do, however, remember how I felt in the moments after I gave all that I knew to give of myself to Jesus. It was as if God was holding me and not only that, but He was never going to let me go and that I would always get to be with Him. In my mind this meant I was going to get to go to heaven when I died, but in my being it meant so much more. The whole experience was probably explained best in these words: God was there and so was I and no matter what, God would always be there and so would I. The only words that could even come close to expressing my experience at that time were, "I'm going to heaven." Four simple, maybe over-used, words in Christianity today and yet during that moment they made so much sense.

When my parents decided to stop following the desires of this world and follow all that they knew of Jesus with their lives, they broke a chain of alcoholism, drug addiction and a list of other addictions that would only leave one reading this book in amazement at the miraculous rescuing power of God. I am ever so thankful to my parents and the pastor that kept knocking on their door, for refusing to believe that when in desperate need of an intervention, a needy person must remain locked inside of their own castle. For my parents the whispers of Jesus, through one man, finally broke through the walls and into their minds, causing them to dream and never again wake up. Because of my parents, leaving their castles of loneliness and self-saturation, I was born into an ever-so-freeing land where I quickly learned this was the place in which I belonged.

I remember playing cops and robbers, or a similar type of game, with my sister Kelly when I was little where one person would catch the other person and force them to remain locked up in a sort of imaginary prison. Usually, I was the robber and ended up getting caught by my sister and stuck in an unbreakable, imaginary cell. When I was the cop I could seldom catch my sister, but if I did, I definitely could not keep her in prison. There was something about my sister's mind that worked differently than mine. Every time that I managed to catch her we would get into some kind of argument that consisted of me first saying she could not get out of prison. Kelly would respond by claiming she had a secret key. I would reply that the door had more than one lock. She would simply claim her secret key opened all locks. I would say the door was electrified so if she touched it, even with a key, she would die. She would argue her key was rubber so she would therefore be protected from the electric current. I would say that the current was too strong and she would die for sure. Kelly would say that she was wearing an anti-electricity suit that could withstand all electrical shock. I would say it wasn't heavy enough to stop the current. Kelly would retort that of course it was heavy enough, it was the heaviest suit in the world. I would respond by saying that was good because even if she did get through the electric prison door, the moat around the prison was so deep and her suit was so heavy she would drown if she tried to leave.

Kelly would laugh as she ran away from my imaginary prison shouting over her shoulder that I was unaware of the flying capabilities of this special suit. No matter how hard I tried to keep my sister in prison, she would not stay. I wondered for a while if all this was because she had a far greater imagination than I did or if she really did not want to stay cooped up in an imaginary space? I eventually figured out it was the latter.

In truth Kelly and I had similar imaginations and played together all the time. If we weren't fighting with my Ninja Turtles, then we were running around with sticks as I was The Flash and she was Laura Ingalls Wilder. Whenever we did play the chasing games, the reason I always ended up in prison and Kelly escaped was simple: she knew what she wanted. She wanted to escape and she wanted to be free. In fact, Kelly usually let me catch her so she could run away from me laughing.

I, on the other hand, when caught, felt I needed to convince Kelly of my freedom and be free in her mind before I could actually be free in my own. Being my older sister, she was not easily persuaded by my poorly constructed arguments. Of course this was only two children playing childish games, but every time we played, my sister was free because she wanted to be and I was, at most, only trying hard to be free. My freedom was contingent upon someone else's mind and my sister understood the real rules of the game. Thus the game was hers and she controlled where she wanted to run. I could not tell her to stay in prison if she did not want to be there and cooperate. We both knew this truth extremely well and this truth, discovered by two children on some farmland in Idaho, was what ultimately set me free from some of the imaginary prisons I discovered later in life.

This all began when my parents, a year before my birth, escaped their castle walls and learned a life of freedom. Not freedom from sinning, but freedom from sin and the ungracious consequences of shame, guilt, fear, addiction and death, which rose out of Adam, Eve and the rest of my parents' previous generations. I grew up, figuratively, in a free forest and although some days it felt more like a prison because of the walls I unknowingly attempted to construct within my own mind, I was free and no one, not even I, could steal this freedom. My rhythm was shaky. I was a slow learner. Jesus had injected Himself, through my parents, into my life and had begun teaching me how to dance.

24

Sex

Once I heard someone say the Bible is a book completely about relationships. Then that person began quoting Genesis 1:1 saying, "In the beginning ... relationship." I like the idea of God creating the world and humans around the idea of relationship. I do not so much like the thought of our messing it up so fast, but I love it that God was not finished with us just because we wanted to be selfish. He kept loving us and (since we were not the best receivers of His love) has spent the rest of human history, calling us back to be in relationship with Him. Some people even say the Bible is a love letter to all of humanity from God. I think of the Bible more as a book of stories that point out God's character, our flawed character and His love which transcends our inability to relate with holiness, making it possible for us to be in relationship.

Think about God wanting to be in relationship with us. I keep wondering why He would want that. Some say God is lonely without humans so that is why He created us. I do not really like that idea and if it is true, why do you suppose Jesus, when He was on earth, spent so much time trying to be alone with His Father, away from people? Ultimately, I do not believe God is lonely without us and honestly, I have no idea why He would take the time to create people who even have the slightest potential to reject Him – unless God really loves the idea of relationship.

By this I mean, God loves the idea of relationship so much He dared create us knowing He was going to be rejected by us. In fact, God has been in relationship since the beginning. After all, God is the beginning and if it is true that God is not only Father but also Son and Holy Spirit then God has been in constant relationship with that which, although Himself, is also separate from Himself and capable of being in community with each part of who God is. Perhaps God loves this idea of being in relationship so much He knew He must share it with something that one day might appreciate it as much at it would appreciate Him and His inexplicable existence. Maybe God did not separate Himself from the idea of relationship at all and in that way made it possible for us to come and relate to Him. Maybe God created us so that we could enjoy Him, through relationship, in the same way that He has been enjoying Himself through relationship, since before time began. What if we were created for nothing more than to enjoy God by sharing in a part of Him that cannot be separated from Him and yet can be shared with all those who come to Him and in that way become present to a relationship that is meant to be experienced in the same way as the Holy Trinity.

Sometimes I wonder if God was actually experiencing romantic relationship before He created humans and for that matter, before He created time. In all honesty, when I think about sex, I think of a moment where two people are simultaneously experiencing each other and hopefully fully aware and able to perceive what is happening between them. For God to be three-in-one means that when He is three persons He is also one and although He is being one with the other two persons, He is still three. To me this all sounds extremely sexual and I think that is okay. Even more than okay, I think that our ability to better understand the relationship of God to Himself and us through sexual intercourse is good.

God said in Genesis 2:18 it was not good for Adam, the first man, to be alone. I think this statement is important to our understanding for two reasons. First, God did not say it was bad Adam was alone, He said that it was not good. We automatically assume this means Adam being alone was bad, but obviously God was not thinking this way. The only reason any of this matters is because too many people believe God is constantly sitting up in heaven looking for the bad in people instead of knowing what is good and working toward that end. God saw good and wanted to make all He had created able to experience the good that He knew. Second, this could be why God created Eve. Maybe He saw Adam could experience the goodness He knew by providing Him with Eve so two people might become one, as He was one while at the same time they would still be two, like God was three. If this is true, all of it happened just as much for Eve as it did for Adam. Basically, this posits that God created Adam and Eve to experience each other sexually so they could better understand Him, His relationship to Himself and also to them.

Sometimes I wonder if it is possible to comprehend even a small part of God outside of the concepts of sex, without getting skewed in our beliefs. For instance, we have many different denominations, all of which base their identities on some understood characteristic which God is believed to possess. Some denominations base their entire theology of God on the premise that He is eternally sovereign and therefore reach far-out "logical" conclusions which leave some people wondering if God can really be love. These denominations might respond to opposition of doctrine by telling others that instead of themselves having a skewed view of God these "others" have a skewed view of love. This works vice-versa with many other different belief systems depending on the denomination. What if understanding God began with knowing Him, sitting at His feet and not trying to make Him fit into our heads, but rather attempting to embrace wholly all God has provided for us so we could more fully understand Him by experiencing all the good God created us to experience?

When I was a child I sometimes had the tendency to be annoying. I know, given my super-mature character today, I probably was not too annoying as a kid, but nonetheless, I did have my days. Just kidding. I recall bothering my mother by asking her again and again if I could have something to eat. Usually the conversation went something like this (and I always did the majority of the talking): "Mom, can I have a cookie? Mom, can I have a cookie? Mom, can I have a cookie? Mom! Mom! Mom!" "Rod," she would say. "Can I have a cookie?" I would respond. In that moment Mom would always say one of the wisest sayings I have ever heard in my life (I learned a great deal from asking my mother for cookies): "Roderick Morrell Tucker, if you ask me for a cookie one more time, I will be about ready, myself, to cookie you."

I always understood exactly what she was saying. Okay, so the story did not always go exactly like that, but I did learn to understand what different words meant at different times by understanding the context in which my mother was using them. Sometimes Mom was about to "fork" me, if I was playing with the kitchen utensils. Other times I found myself in great danger of being "cookie-doughed" or even "saladed" if I stuck around too long in the kitchen with my fingers in the food. But I understood what she was saying, because she chose words intended to drive home a point – which also usually got me out of the way. So when Jesus says that He is the Truth (Jn 14:6), He is making a greater claim than just arguing that He is a collaboration of solid facts. What Jesus was trying to explain that when everything boils down to what really matters, He is reality, the One who gives our lives meaning, purpose and even makes us real.

When Jesus claimed to be the truth, He was claiming He could make us authentic and that the way in which we could understand what was happening was through the concepts of oneness, unity and physical intimacy in marriage. Think about John 8:32 when Jesus says that we, "will know the truth and the truth will set [us] free." The word that He uses for "know" is *ginosko* which means in some contexts "to have sexual relations". While I doubt Jesus was telling us to have sex with the truth, I do believe He was making a point, just like my mother used to make, through her choice of words. Jesus might have been telling us we are going to know Him as reality in a deeper way than we have ever experienced, maybe even in a way that will transcend our own individual experience and bring us into a place that can only begin to be understood through analogies such as marital union or fairy tales about princesses.

By all this I am not saying God is somehow in some sort of sexual relationship with Himself and with us, as we understand sex. However, because analogy is the greatest way to understand that which is holy or divine in a realm that is wholly neither, I wonder constantly if physical intimacy in a marriage relationship is one of the best analogies to understand God and His relationship to Himself and us that we have in our human experience.

One thing that I notice, especially in young people today, is that a twisted view of sex promotes a twisted view of God. I see two different ways to view sex in our culture: sex as performance and sex as physical intimacy. We constantly see sex being depicted as performance-based in our culture – which means if anyone is not good at sex, then they cannot have good sex. A recent rap song speaks of how a man claims to be in love with a stripper because she can do things with her body that supposedly shame ordinary women. The way she dances, moves her body and looks is better, according to this song – which evidently attempts to prove that sex is about performance so this man is in love because this stripper can make him feel good.

This may be an extreme case, but sex in our culture is being

Remembering a Forgotten Grace

twisted to be solely a performance-based experience. However, if physical intimacy is truly one of the best analogies we have to understand God and His relationship to us, then obviously viewing sex as only for pleasure might cause one to see God as not desiring physical intimacy, but rather wanting to please us, or make us feel good by what He does and vice-versa with us doing good deeds and not doing bad ones. This skewed view of sex for pleasure leads naturally to a performance-based Christianity. Where sex is viewed as physical intimacy there is the possibility that those who experience this type of union might more easily understand God as One who desires an intimate, deep connection with all individuals, not just pleasing appearances and right actions.

At this point grace comes into play. I always love it when this all-empowering force steps up to the plate. I believe in the deepest part of everyone's heart, even those who have made sexual mistakes against their own bodies in the past, there is a desire to be intimate with God, a passion to be swept off of our feet and be Christ's bride. Thus, God longs to become our Groom and to whisper into our ears that He loves us no matter what and God is waiting, just like He has always been, to share a deeply intimate relationship with us. Such an experience is far greater than any previously sought-for pleasure. God is calling us to be real – with each other, with Him and with those who do not know what it means to be continually and unchangingly new. God is longing to pull all people together under His powerful arms, by the grace of His Son, and tell us that He loves everything about who we are and have become. This God wants to open our eyes so we can see our true selves, one with God, becoming one with each other, as His church. Once we are God's church this realness lasts.

25

Trust

I once worked for a youth residential counseling facility which helped teenagers and their families who were struggling with various issues through a Christ-centered, year-long program. We temporarily removed students between the ages of 14 and 18 from their families and placed them in a residential setting, allowing them, with counselors and residential staff, to work on issues and decisions that were taking these students to places they did not want to be. I shared a house with three male staff and seven boys.

One day I was talking with a resident who was upset with some of the other staff with whom he had become close during his stay and he explained how these individuals aggravated him and that he was sick of people confronting him in the ways they were doing. We discussed this dilemma for a time and then I had one of my crazy ideas. I told him to follow me and I led him to the edge of the dock on our small pond. He quickly obliged when I told him we were going to the dock because we had had several significant conversations there. This time we did not sit and talk for an hour or so. In fact, we did not stay on the dock for more than five minutes.

I told him to move toward the edge of the dock so his toes would hang over the edge. That was the easy part. Then I asked him to close his eyes. When he did I began to push him over the edge of the dock while only holding the back of his shirt with two of my fingers. I let him know I was holding him by the shirt with my fingers and as he was freaking out I asked, "Is this enough, or would you feel safer if I had a better grip?" He, very calmly, told me he would prefer if I had a better grip. Just kidding. This kid was starting to get real scared. I then placed a hand on his shoulder, pushed him out a little further and asked him the same question. He responded by wanting me to grab him harder. So I did. I put both my hands on his arms and squeezed hard, holding him out over the water and asking if his arms hurt. When he said yes, I asked if he would prefer if I loosened my grip. He said no, so I asked if he felt safer although he was in more pain than before. He said yes again and I responded by telling him that sometimes what hurts most in life is when people refuse to let us drown. I then asked if he was ready to trust what we were doing although it was upsetting him. He tried to answer, but I did not let him. This question needed more time than he was willing to give. I went inside and let him think.

Sometimes I wonder how many of us do with God what this young man was doing with some of his closest relationships. Truth be told, he did not know what he needed in order to begin making good decisions. He might have thought he did, but he was completely wrong. He had been brought to this place so we might have a chance to stop him from ending up in a place that he does not want to be. Because of this dynamic, our job was to help him do things he did not want to do while, at the same time, not letting him do things which are unhealthy that he wants to do. This will help him reach the place where he truly wants to be.

I believe many of us are like this young man. We want one thing, but God is doing something better and we complain. We desire to be with a certain person, but God is preparing us for someone who will bless us more than anyone else in the world;

still we complain. We want a certain amount of money, but God wants to give it to someone who really needs it and we complain. Ultimately, I wonder if we all need to take a trip down to the dock with God and begin to understand that through all of the hard things that happen to us in life, He is holding us tightly and is not going to let us drown. This is what I am learning. To be in the hand of God is not a ride in a gondola with gentle waters below and the love of your life by your side. Being in God's hand is more like flying over an erupting volcano in a helicopter you must learn to trust is never going to crash. Giving our lives to Christ is intense, but we know He is not going to let us drown.

In Matthew 14:29 Jesus tells Peter not to focus on circumstances, fix his eyes on Him and walk on water all with one word: Come. And Peter does just that! Sure, he starts to sink and needs help from Jesus, but he walks on water! How many of us could physically walk on water if our eyes were fixed on Jesus? Although I've never seen anyone do it, for some reason I still believe it to be possible. Even more than that, how many of us could stand on top of all of the sadness, fear, shame, guilt and pain in our lives if we could look past our circumstances and see Jesus? He is not going to let us drown. This is where we must learn to trust. "[He] will keep in perfect peace him whose mind is steadfast, because he trusts in You" (Is 26:3).

Trusting God and standing up in the midst of pain is difficult because with God we do not always have the opportunity to see what is happening. Trusting God to heal my pain is different than trusting my dad to get me cookies out of the cupboard. I can watch my dad do that, but I cannot necessarily see God heal my pain. With God, healing might happen but I do not notice it until after-the-fact. I have noticed in reading the Bible that God's people tend only to see what God has done after it happens. Noah did not see a rainbow being created in the sky. He saw a rainbow that had already been created and it was brilliant. In Genesis we read

Remembering a Forgotten Grace

that God created the world by speaking yet we do not know what happened between those moments when God said, "Let there be" and when that whatever came into being. We do not know how God does what He does, but we do know when we come to Him openly and honestly He gives us rest. We may not know how, but we know He does. This is why we must learn to trust. The Bible says to, "Trust in the LORD with all your heart and lean not on your own understanding" (Prv 3:5). This is a new kind of trust. Relationship with Jesus involves trust that keeps focused on Him, even when the circumstances, like the waves, are high.

I know I do not always have this trust when it comes to my circumstances and God. However, one statement I can make is that whether I trusted God or not in the moments I found myself in pain, things always worked out better than I thought they would if I did not get my way. And usually I did not get my way. Ultimately I feel God is bringing me to a place where I can soundly believe that, no matter what happens, I will be okay. Even if my circumstances are difficult and I feel like giving up, because God is not going to let me drown, I will be okay. By this I mean I will always be with the One who loves me the most. Joyfully, I am learning to be okay with that.

26

Joy

I used to think that finding freedom and joy was similar to arriving at the top of what had previously seemed to be an insurmountable mountain. I believed if I struggled hard enough I would eventually pull myself over the last boulder and drink from this always satisfying fountain of joy. I tried and tried to climb this mountain, but no matter how much my striving proved to be praiseworthy to myself and others, I always fell short of this freedom. I ended up deciding, after several desperate lunges in the wrong direction, that joy was more of a mirage in a desert of perpetual sadness and incessant failure than it was a mountain which I was climbing. I did not know how to find joy and giving up was looking pretty good. Then one day I read something in the book of Joel that caught my attention:

"Even now," declares the Lord, "return to me with all your heart, with fasting and weeping and mourning."... Then the Lord will be jealous for His land and take pity on His people. The Lord will reply to them: "I am sending you grain, new wine and oil, enough to satisfy you fully; never again will I make you an object of scorn to the nations." Be glad, O people of Zion, rejoice in the Lord your God, for He has given you the autumn rains in righteousness. He sends you abundant showers... "I will repay you for the years the locusts have eaten" (Joel 2:12, 18-19, 23, 25a).

Remembering a Forgotten Grace

It's useful to remember the book of Joel was written during a time of great drought. The people not only needed rain, but plagues of locusts had been sweeping through crops, devouring what they had been working so hard to grow and needed in order to survive. This concept of repayment was incredibly striking to me when I read that God wanted Israel to return to Him with all of its heart and then He would give them rain and repay Israel for the years the locusts had eaten. Did God owe Israel anything? Of course not. So why was He saying if they returned to Him with all of their hearts He would repay them for their lost years? Maybe this is like the process of salvation. For some of us salvation confronted us when we were young, but this is not true for everyone. Some people do not find themselves colliding into the grace of God until they are much older. What is the difference between those who find themselves trying to live lives which exemplify Christ because they met Him at an early age and those who meet Him later, after leading a life of extraordinary pain, shame, guilt and selfishness?

These two types of people are at opposite ends of what we might see as a salvation spectrum. But what is the discrepancy between these two seemingly extreme cases? Perhaps they are like the locusts. Imagine the dissimilar amount of debt between a four-year-old boy and his father. The boy may obviously have no more debt to society than to be thankful to his parents for continually putting food on the table and tucking him in at night. On the other hand, the boy's father may have college loans, a car payment and a second mortgage on his house. Imagine that an extremely generous philanthropist comes along and says she will pay off the greater of these two debts. Which would you say is greater? I might argue the boy's debt is far greater than his father's because of the relationship involved, but my argument would prove to be pointless because unconditional relationships, more than likely, do not remember debt. Therefore, it is obvious the father's debt is far greater than his son's and this particular philanthropist is undoubtedly going to be stuck with several large bills.

Don't get me wrong. I am not claiming, in regards to sin and salvation, that some people's sin is greater than other's and that they need more grace and forgiveness in order to be made right with God. Nevertheless, in consideration of the lack of rain and plethora of locusts in some people's lives, some individuals are in a greater need of repayment for all of what appears to be a wasted life. This is where grace becomes an all-important equalizer. The father receives unmerited favor. His debt is paid. In respect to money owed, he and his son are equal, so it would seem this father owes the same to the philanthropist as his son owes to him -- thankfulness. There is no difference between those who know Christ early in life and those who meet Him later. All are repaid for what has been lost and eaten and all are thankful. Joel also says God is able to satisfy us fully no matter how many years the locusts have eaten from our lives. He is able to repay us for those years. All we must do is come to Him with undivided hearts. How do we do that? By going before Christ and sitting at His feet, fasting, weeping and mourning and, when all has become silent, perceiving an estimate of God's grace in heed of our circumstances.

This is not a step-by-step process to discover joy in one's life. This is my experience and a great benefit of life is that my stories can be shared with you and your stories can be shared with me. As a result of this community, we can come closer to apprehending the heart of God and thus know Him for more of who He says He is through His writing of our stories. Ultimately, it is God who authors these works. We are like vials of ink into which He dips His pen in order to create masterpieces from that which can only be called pools of joyless black ink with no potential – except in the mind of someone who cares. Personally, I believe it is time we all approach God with repentant hearts, acknowledging that we looked in other places in attempts of finding His joy. The time is now that we pursue Jesus with undivided hearts, shedding those things which call out our names to entice us to look for satisfaction elsewhere.

The Old Testament tells of times when other nations, such as the Philistines, confronted Israel, claiming that God is nothing. During those times the Israelites usually stood in fear, unable to move, until one person, with an undivided heart, stands in the gap for God and, consequently, an entire nation (see 1 Samuel 17). There are times when kings like Nebuchadnezzar claim to worship no other god than the God of Israel, because three men with undivided hearts found themselves unharmed and walking inside a fiery furnace (see Daniel 3). These stories make me long to have an undivided heart for God, because the more I apprehend the heart of God, the more I understand His heart is the heart He wants me to have. Even though joy is not the reason I pursue God's heart, I am learning that this kind of satisfaction can only come through an intimate relationship with Him. For me to be in true relationship with Jesus, I cannot be trying other things, just as I cannot sleep around with other women after I have become one with my bride. This is God's call on my life and although I will make mistakes, I can now live in a land where I will always have the opportunity to feature, before Jesus, an undivided heart. This is my desire. This is my story.

When I was a child my mom left home and checked herself into a treatment center for co-dependency. I thought the reason she left was my fault, as if I had done something wrong. I was sad when my family and I had to celebrate my birthday at the facility, because I wanted my family to be normal and for my mom to be okay. I wondered constantly if there were something I could do to make things right or if there were something I had done to make things wrong. I lived in a society where my family was considered to be the very people that were wrong with all the families of the world, because we were honest about our problems and somehow we were attempting to work our way back to normalcy. What I did not know at the time was that this was how everyone feels at one time or another.

Sometimes I wonder if we live our lives as though we are outside of our own bodies, watching our experiences and judging the ways in which we perform, as though we were in a circus. Maybe we live like this because we want to be able to say that we tried our best when others tell us that all of our strivings have fallen short, or perhaps it's because we want to see ourselves fail and then feel that pain just so we can know we are alive. Maybe neither is the reason and maybe we will never know.

One thing I do know is that pain comes in peculiar ways and usually we do not recognize the hurt when we get hit. The first time a girl ended a relationship with me in high school I assumed that what I felt was what I was intended to feel because, in my mind, I believed I was a reject, one meant to be rejected. I did not think I was good at basketball because people told me I was not. I definitely did not believe I was the smartest kid in my class because all of the tests told me otherwise. I was not the best looking because it seemed like none of the girls wanted to talk to me. I felt like I was some kind of a freak, slowly working my way back to normality, wanting to be loved by those who, I came to find out later, were just like me.

To think that all of the kids in my high school wanted to be loved like I wanted to be loved was crazy when the idea first hit me. I learned the truth was not so much that everyone thought I was abnormal, but that everyone was striving to be something everyone else might someday love. We all wanted to hear those words, "I love you no matter what," but we did not know if we would truly believe the "no matter what" part.

It wasn't until I found myself, at age twenty-three, sitting in a mini-van with a pastor friend of mine telling him of my passion

Remembering a Forgotten Grace

for those who have been rejected and hearing him say the words, "present passions are windows to past wounds," that I began to pray and ask God what my biggest wound was. I went back to my room after our brief afternoon conversation and wrote down on a piece of paper, "God, what is the lie that I am hearing?" Then I waited. I waded through some of my own thoughts and then I heard the answer to my question: "You are a reject. You are meant to be rejected and nothing more. You are of inferior quality." I had never previously heard anyone call me a reject, or tell me I was of inferior quality in those exact words, but when I heard them for the first time in that room I knew this lie was what I had been living my life under for the longest time.

Hearing those words brought tears to my eyes because I understood in that moment how much they meant to me. These words, telling me that I was a reject, had been a driving force in my life since I was little. Then I also knew how much I hated those words. I wanted nothing more than to take them captive and make them obedient to Christ who had set me free, because I had been unknowingly captive to them for so long.

The next sentence I wrote on my piece of paper was: "God what is the truth?" I waited and then I heard, "Rod, you are Joseph, my favored one. I love you more than the others." At first I felt weird hearing God say I was favored and loved more than the others, but then it hit me. I had lived my life treading through immense amounts of shame that not only did I not know where it all came from but that had been controlling what I believed about myself. God was telling me the truth about who I was, which was exactly opposite of what I had been hearing my entire life. I was God's chosen one, favored and loved more than the others, just as Joseph's father, in the Bible, loved him the most. I was Joseph and that was how God saw me. I don't fully know how to explain what happened in that moment. There were no flashes of lightening and no powerful clouds of smoke. All I can say is that a door opened.

Although I could not see this door, it was definitely an entrance into something greater in my life, like a moment when you have an epiphany, change your mind about an idea, or realize for the first time you love someone. A door opened and it was a door to a freedom beyond all freedom I knew. Yet instead of walking through this door and realizing that all was well and I had arrived at some sort of self-awareness, I have not stopped walking and I believe I am still in this doorway today. When I told my sister what had happened she bought me a rainbow "What Would Jesus Do" bracelet, not because it said, "what would Jesus do," but because it was colorful, like the coat that Joseph's dad gave to him because he was favored, a beautiful reminder.

I cannot say I do not struggle with feelings of inadequacy anymore or that shame never taps on my window. However, one thing I can say from experience is that when a person knows the truth about himself, he is free and he can only become freer each day he lives with the One who has carried him away from his old dreams and into an unchanging newness. I no longer desire to become an individual of great success or righteousness. What I long for is freedom. This is not a freedom that has me doing anything to prove I am free, but a freedom that will come only when I have been brought to a place that transcends my experience, a place where you and I and God are one. Personally I believe I am already but not yet in that place and I am learning to be okay with this limbo, because Philippians 1:3 says that Christ's work will undoubtedly be completed.

This will be a place where analogies are no longer needed, because we will be in a never-ending and new moment for all eternity. We will be free and we will understand. I long for that day like the moon longs for the light of the sun, like the dreams of a princess long for the freedom of an open forest. I long for the day when you and I will be together in unity and we will see His face. Until then let us be that which we can only understand by the constant re--defining of the word grace and let us love each other like we desire to be loved. We are the body of Christ and one day we will know fully, as we are fully known. I long for that day, but I can wait, because I know today is a taste of what will be. Every morning is a glimpse of the joy we will share. Every breath is a taste of the life we are beginning to truly live each moment we are aware of His presence in what appears to be the most unholy of places.

I heard once that the priests' main jobs in the Old Testament was to distinguish the uncommon from the common, the divine from the ordinary, or in other words, the holy from the unholy. I like this idea, mainly because Christ has set us apart. We are now holy and not only that, we are the new priests. I think that life in Christ's body can be seen by all as a good thing if we began to distinguish that which has come into our everyday (Christ) and thus know that it is Jesus Christ who makes all things new. There is no difference between you and me if we know the truth.

Without further elaboration, it is with great privilege I present to you, once again, the grace and hope of our Lord and Savior. May He sweep you off of your feet, tell you the name which He has been longing to call you and whisper into your ear the words you have desired to hear for the longest time. Let Him do that for you. Jesus must become of more worth to you than your own concepts of love. For it is He who loves you and He loves you no matter what.

I've heard that the word "amen" means, "let it be done." So to all of this story we have shared together, to all of the shame we have confronted, to all of the grace we have apprehended and to all of the romance we have yet to experience with our Savior, I say amen. Let it be done. Let us be free. Let us love each other in community. Let us share our stories of healing. Let us speak with the words of God and let those words be full of grace. Let us live in the truth that Jesus will always be in the places where we need Him and never in the places that we do not. Let us always acknowledge our need for Jesus. Let us come to God continually, under His all-encompassing blanket of grace and acceptance and let us witness His glory in the way we have been, since the beginning of time, intended to witness it, with undivided hearts. Let this be done. "Grace be with all those who love our Lord Jesus Christ in sincerity. Amen" (Eph 6:24).

Epilogue

We live in a shame-based, commercialistic-minded culture which tells us constantly we are screwed up if we do not own the right shoes or car. We are almost consumers by nature and although our desire to consume has failed extravagantly in its attempts to make us complete individuals, we continue pursuing our desires (like Adam and Eve, the most primitive of our ancestors) either to be like God, or at least make it so no one else knows we are naked and lacking. The truth is that we are all naked and lacking. We are all in need of relationships which can look at our hearts, spread out on the table and say "I love you anyway. In fact, I love you always. I love you no matter what." We find this relationship in Christ at first and then hopefully later in His body, which is us but not in the same sense that we have always thought of us.

Usually we think in terms of you and me, but the concept of us must become an understanding of us in order to further apprehend how the body of Christ is truly intended to function in our world. This all may seem incredibly philosophical, but please know it is more practical than anything else. We must be together to know we are all okay, otherwise we will always view ourselves as "the only one." We must be together and we must be unconditional as best we know how. We are all naked and lacking, but together we may realize there is no need to consume every marketing strategy individually, whether it be figurative or literal stuff, placed on our plates. We must cross the threshold of attempting to fix ourselves and learn to love. We must begin transcending ourselves through participation in the practical body of Christ and learn to love. We must become less of us and more of Jesus. We must love, because God is love and in Him there is no lacking for anyone. Finally we must love because love is what we were created to do. We must shake off all of our fears that have kept us from jumping off the roof of our lives and into an unconditional realm of love and we must jump. Ultimately, we must know that where there is perfect love there is no fear and where there is no fear there is no shame and in that place of no shame and no fear there is only grace and because of grace we can honestly know we are in a place where we have truly sought the Lord.

Bibliography

Anderson, Neil T., Rich Miller and Paul Travis. *Breaking the Bondage of Legalism.* Eugene, OR: Harvest House Publishers, 2003.

Lewis, C. S. *The Weight of Glory.* New York, NY: HarperSanFransisco, 2001.

Miller, Donald. *Searching for God Knows What.* Nashville, TN: Nelson Books, 2004.

Moore, Beth. *Breaking Free: Making Liberty in Christ a Reality in Life.* Nashville, TN: Broadman & Holman Publishers, 2000.

Additional copies of this book may be obtained
from your bookstore
or by contacting
Hope Publishing House
P.O. Box 60008
Pasadena, CA 91116 - U.S.A.
(626) 792-6123 / (800) 326-2671
Fax (626) 792-2121
E-mail: hopepub@sbcglobal.net
www.hope-pub.com